MEMENTO
&
FOLLOWING

D1530220

MEMENTO
&
FOLLOWING
Christopher Nolan

ff

faber and faber

Faber and Faber, Inc.
An affiliate of Farrar, Straus and Giroux
18 West 18th Street, New York 10011

Printed in the United States of America
Originally published in 2001 by Faber and Faber Limited,
3 Queen Square, London WC1N 3AU
Published in the United States by Faber and Faber, Inc.
First American edition, 2001

A CIP record for this book is available from the British Library
Library of Congress Control Number: 2003427846

ISBN-13: 978-0-571-21047-3
ISBN-10: 0-571-21047-3

www.fsgbooks.com

6   8   10   12   13   11   9   7

This book would not have been possible without the generous support and
cooperation of Aaron Ryder and the Newmarket Capital Group.
Furthermore, the contribution of Emma Thomas was inestimable.

CONTENTS

Following

CAST AND CREW

MAIN CAST

THE YOUNG MAN	Jeremy Theobald
COBB	Alex Haw
THE BLONDE	Lucy Russell
THE POLICEMAN	John Nolan
THE BALD GUY	Dick Bradsell
THE HOMEOWNER	Gillian El-Kadi
THE WAITRESS	Jennifer Angel
BARMAN	Nicolas Carlotti
ACCOUNTANT	Darren Ormandy
HEAVY #1	Guy Greenway
HEAVY #2	Tassos Stevens
MAN AT BAR	Tristan Martin
WOMAN AT BAR	Rebecca James
HOMEOWNER'S HUSBAND	Paul Mason
HOMEOWNER'S FRIEND	David Bovill

MAIN CREW

Directed by	Christopher Nolan
Written by	Christopher Nolan
Produced by	Christopher Nolan
	Jeremy Theobald
	Emma Thomas
Original Music by	David Julyan
Cinematography by	Christopher Nolan
Film Editing by	Gareth Heal
	Christopher Nolan
Production Design by	Tristan Martin

EXT. CROWDED LONDON STREET — DAY

An endless stream of pedestrians crossing the frame.

Cut to a shot, looking through pedestrians and reflections of pedestrians, of a Young Man sitting in the window of a coffee shop, looking out at the people walking past.

> MALE VOICE (V.O.)
> The following is my explanation . . . well, my . . . my account of . . . well, what happened.

The Young Man is tall and slim, mid- to late twenties, with dark, long, greasy hair and unshaven.

We cut to the Young Man outside, on the street. He is peering ahead as he walks, as if trying to spot a lost friend.

> I'd, ah, been on my own for quite a while by then and I'd become . . . lonely . . .

A wide shot shows the Young Man amidst a bustling Oxford Street crowd.

> . . . and bored. Nothing to do all day, you see. That's when I began shadowing.

> OLDER MALE VOICE (V.O.)
> Shadowing?

> MALE VOICE (V.O.)
> Yeah, shadowing, following. I started to follow people.

The Young Man cuts purposefully through the crowd in slo-mo.

> OLDER MALE VOICE (V.O.)
> Who?

> MALE VOICE (V.O.)
> Anyone, a stranger. I mean that was the whole point: follow-

3

ing someone completely at random. Anyone who wouldn't know who you were.

The Young Man is staring at someone fixedly as he moves in slo-mo. His POV shows us a man's back dodging between other people, always threatening to lose us, still in slo-mo.

OLDER MALE VOICE (V.O.)

And then?

MALE VOICE (V.O.)

And then nothing.

We snap into real time. The man's back disappears into the crowd and we cease to follow him. The noises of the city come up loud.

The Young Man has come to a virtual standstill. He watches the world washing around him.

OLDER MALE VOICE (V.O.)

Nothing?

MALE VOICE (V.O.)

Nothing. I'd follow somebody for a while then pick someone else and follow them or go home or whatever.

The Young Man's eyes dart about, watching the people around him. He starts to wander down the road, pulled gently by the flow of pedestrians.

OLDER MALE VOICE (V.O.)

Why did you do it?

MALE VOICE (V.O.)

How can I explain? Your eyes pass over the crowd . . .

We pan across endless anonymous faces.

. . . and if you let them settle on a person, then that person becomes an individual . . .

We fix on a face, a woman hurrying along.

. . . just . . . like . . . THAT . . .

Shock cut on the sound of snapping fingers at 'THAT' to:

INT. ROOM WITH TABLE — DAY

Close on fingers in front of the Young Man's face. He looks different: hair short, clean-shaven, bruised face, a plaster over one eye. Seated opposite is an Older Man.

> YOUNG MAN
>
> It just became . . . irresistible.

The Older Man considers this before replying.

> OLDER MAN
> (*suspicious*)
>
> So you followed women?

> YOUNG MAN
>
> It wasn't some sex thing. I followed anyone. Just for the sake of it, just to see where they went, what they were doing.

> OLDER MAN
>
> You were playing secret agent.

> YOUNG MAN
> (*knows it's true, but doesn't like it*)
>
> No . . . I'm a writer – I want to be a writer. I wanted to gather material for characters, you know, to write about them. All I did was follow people – to begin with.

DISSOLVE TO:

EXT. BUSY STREET IN THE WEST END — DAY

The Young Man (long hair, unshaven) exits a café and stumbles along the road. His eye is caught by a man passing by in the opposite direction. The man is in his mid-twenties, tall, dark-haired, wearing a dark suit. He is carrying an overnight bag.

> YOUNG MAN (V.O.)
>
> I spotted the dangers soon enough. I could tell I was hooked and I made up rules.

The Young Man turns about and starts to follow, speeding up so as not to lose the fast-moving Dark Suit.

Dark Suit weaves in and out of other pedestrians, his bag slung over his shoulder, heavy.

. . . I wouldn't let myself follow anyone for too long. I wouldn't follow women after dark, stuff like that, simple things just to keep it all under control.

The Young Man follows, coming up behind Dark Suit as he waits at a crossing. The lights change and they head across the road, the Young Man hanging back slightly.

Dark Suit enters Charing Cross station, the Young Man in pursuit. Dark Suit crosses the station to the left-luggage office, where he hands his bag to the attendant behind the counter and takes his ticket. He heads back out of the station. The Young Man follows.

Dark Suit enters a small doorway between two shops. The Young Man hangs around near by, before walking up to the doorway and examining the doorbells. The bells are for flats up above the shops; most of the names are not marked. He crosses the road and looks up at the windows, but can't see much through any of them. The Young Man shrugs and starts to walk away, but he hears a door open behind him and he glances back to see Dark Suit coming out of a doorway carrying another overnight bag.

The most important rule was that even if I found out where a person worked or lived, I would *never* follow the same person twice.

Dark Suit looks about as he comes out on to the pavement, and the Young Man is forced to turn back and continue to walk in the direction in which he was already headed. When he reaches the corner, he glances back down the street, but the street is empty. The Young Man looks around thoughtfully before hurrying off around the corner.

The Young Man rushes through crowded streets, not quite running but faster than we've seen him move before.

He rushes into Charing Cross station and stands across from the left-luggage office, waiting breathlessly. Commuters stream across the station, obscuring his view of the office.

Through a gap in the flow of people the Young Man catches a glimpse of Dark Suit. The Young Man moves closer, wading through commuters to get a better look.

He sees Dark Suit hand over his ticket and pick up his first overnight bag.

Dark Suit slings one bag over each shoulder before heading off through the station towards the back entrance on to Hungerford Bridge.

The Young Man follows. They cross the footbridge, trains rumbling past on the right-hand side, the sky darkening.

They pass through the South Bank Centre and head south, entering residential streets as it gets dark. Dark Suit arrives at a small block of flats and lets himself in. The Young Man sees a light come on in a third-floor window. He makes a note of the address, turns and walks away.

It was the most important rule, so it was the one I broke last.

FADE TO BLACK.

EXT. ROW OF TERRACED TOWNHOUSES – DUSK

The Young Man looks up at a second-floor window. His appearance is dramatically different from the preceding scene: his hair is in a short, ragged near-crew cut, and he now wears an old-fashioned dark suit and tie.

The Young Man walks past the row of houses then doubles back on the opposite side, stopping at a bus stop from which he can see the houses. He reaches into the inside pocket of his jacket and takes out a strip of passport photos. He stares at them, and we see that they are of a young blonde woman, perhaps the same woman who drew the curtains.

One of the front doors opens and the young blonde woman exits. The Young Man glances at the photos in his hand – it is the same young woman.

The Blonde comes out on to the street. She is wearing a long overcoat, a purse under her arm.

The Young Man lets her get slightly ahead before tailing her from the opposite side of the street. The Blonde strides purposefully ahead, not looking around.

As they enter a more crowded West End street, the Young Man allows himself to cross on to the same side and move ever closer.

The Blonde glides through the other pedestrians gracefully and easily. Behind her the Young Man bobs and weaves to keep her in sight.

EXT. SMALL ENTRANCE TO A BASEMENT BAR/CLUB – DUSK

The Young Man approaches and stops outside. The passport photos are still in his hand. He glances at them as he replaces them in his inside pocket. He looks at the stairs down into the club, then looks around, rubbing his face.

FADE TO BLACK.

EXT. STREET IN SOHO – DAY

The Young Man walks down the street, following a middle-aged bald man. The Young Man has short hair and is wearing a suit and tie. He is wearing sunglasses and his lip looks swollen.

Baldy stops and turns into a doorway.

The Young Man comes up and examines the names by the bells. They are all companies/offices.

He looks around, crosses the road and slips into a café.

INT. CAFÉ – DAY

The café is empty apart from a woman on her own reading a book at one of the tables.

The Young Man buys a coffee at the counter and heads over to the table nearest the window. He sips at his coffee and glances out of the window to the building opposite.

He takes his dark glasses off and examines his reflection in the blade of the knife that was sitting on the table. His left eye is horribly bruised and swollen – it looks half-closed. There is a plaster above it, across the eyebrow. His lip is swollen and marked where it has been recently split.

8

The Young Man looks up and sees that the lone woman is staring at him. He puts his sunglasses back on and we:

FADE TO BLACK.

EXT. OUTSIDE A BLOCK OF FLATS IN THE WEST END — DAY

The Young Man stares up at the building, perplexed.

Dark Suit comes out of the building, a sports bag slung over his shoulder. As he walks down the street, the Young Man follows, the throng of people washing around them.

Dark Suit dives into a café.

The Young Man comes abreast of it and looks through the window. The café is crowded; Dark Suit has taken a table near the back, facing away from the door. The Young Man looks about, takes a deep breath and pushes open the door to the café.

INT. CAFÉ — DAY

Five or six tables, mostly occupied. Two men behind the counter making the food, one waitress squeezing between the tables.

The Young Man enters. Keeping an eye on Dark Suit's back, the Young Man slides behind a table.

WAITRESS

Yeah?

YOUNG MAN

Coffee, black.

WAITRESS

You're going to take up one of my tables over lunch with just a coffee?

YOUNG MAN

And chips.

He looks up at the Waitress; she's still there.

And an omelette . . . please.

The Waitress turns and leaves.

9

The Young Man looks over to Dark Suit. The sports bag rests beside Dark Suit's feet. Dark Suit eats; we can't see what.

The Waitress brings the Young Man's food. He plays with it as he considers Dark Suit.

The Young Man gulps at his coffee. Time passes, the other tables change.

Dark Suit gets up, picks up his bag and turns around, moving towards the Young Man.

The Young Man studies his half-eaten omelette intently.

DARK SUIT (O.S.)

Mind if I join you?

The Young Man looks up; Dark Suit is at his elbow, smiling. Dark Suit sits down without waiting for a reply.

DARK SUIT
(matter-of-factly)

Who and why?

The Young Man looks confused. The Waitress is at their table.

(to Waitress)

Another black coffee for me and . . .

(to the Young Man)

. . . what are you having?

The Young Man shakes his head and starts to murmur negatives. Dark Suit reaches over, picks up the Young Man's empty mug and sniffs it.

(to Waitress)

And another coffee . . .

(he looks into the mug)

. . . also black.

The Waitress leaves. Dark Suit stares at the Young Man, who is having trouble returning his gaze.

You're obviously not a policeman, so who are you and why are you following me?

10

The Young Man half-smiles as if he has not understood the question, then glances from side to side in an attempt to look uncomprehending.

YOUNG MAN

I'm sorry?

DARK SUIT

You've been following me all morning . . . why?

YOUNG MAN

Following? I'm sorry but I've absolutely no idea what you're talking about –

DARK SUIT

(*aggressive*)

Don't piss me about. Who the fuck are you?

The Young Man can't think of anything to say. An uncomfortable silence is broken by the Waitress bringing two coffees.

(*to Waitress, eyes still on Young Man*)

Thanks.

(*to Young Man*)

Sugar?

The Young Man shakes his head. Dark Suit breaks eye contact to spoon two sugars into his coffee. He stirs it noisily, looking up expectantly, waiting for the Young Man to speak. The Young Man's mouth opens and closes silently several times before he speaks.

YOUNG MAN

Look, I'm not . . . I haven't been following you, I just . . . I just saw you with your bag and I thought you looked . . . interesting.

DARK SUIT

What are you, a faggot?

YOUNG MAN

No! No, I, I, I'm a . . . Look, I saw you on the street and . . . and you reminded me of someone I went to school with – to tell the truth I thought you were him, so I followed you and came in here – I came in here 'cos I was hungry – but I wanted to see if it was him . . .

Dark Suit stares at him.

(fading)

. . . but it wasn't.

DARK SUIT

Why didn't you just ask me when you saw me?

YOUNG MAN

I would've been embarrassed.

DARK SUIT
(smiling)

Not as embarrassed as you are now.

YOUNG MAN
(laughing nervously)

No, I suppose not.

Dark Suit sips at his coffee. The Young Man follows suit.

DARK SUIT

What's your name?

YOUNG MAN

Bill.

Dark Suit smiles.

DARK SUIT

Well, 'Bill' . . . what do you do?

YOUNG MAN

Actually, I'm kind of –

DARK SUIT

'Between jobs right now.'

YOUNG MAN

That's right.

DARK SUIT

What *would* you do?

YOUNG MAN

I don't know.

                    DARK SUIT
                    (*smiling*)
Don't be coy, 'Bill'. There must be some burning ambition
eating away at you. Some kind of starving artist?

                    YOUNG MAN
No.

                    DARK SUIT
No?

                    YOUNG MAN
No.

                    DARK SUIT
Painter?

                    YOUNG MAN
No.

                    DARK SUIT
Photos?

                    YOUNG MAN
No.

                    DARK SUIT
Films?

                    YOUNG MAN
No.

                    DARK SUIT
Writer?

                    YOUNG MAN
                    (*slight pause*)
No.

                    DARK SUIT
Writer.

                    YOUNG MAN
NO.

DARK SUIT

But you write?

YOUNG MAN

Not really.

DARK SUIT

But sometimes?

YOUNG MAN

Sometimes, who doesn't?

DARK SUIT

Me.

(*pause*)

So you're a writer.

YOUNG MAN

I didn't say that. What makes you think that I'm a writer anyway?

DARK SUIT

Educated, unemployed twentysomething, fancies himself a
writer . . . real leap into the unknown.

YOUNG MAN

Well, I'm not a writer.

DARK SUIT

But you're interested in people.

YOUNG MAN

Yeah.

DARK SUIT

This person?

YOUNG MAN

I suppose –

DARK SUIT

You haven't even asked my name.

YOUNG MAN

What's your –

DARK SUIT

Or what's in my bag.

YOUNG MAN

Bag?

DARK SUIT
(*gestures at his feet*)
My bag. The one you've been staring at.

There is a pause during which Dark Suit stares challengingly at the Young Man, who looks thoughtful, undecided.

YOUNG MAN
(*sighing*)
What's your name and what's in your bag?

Dark Suit smiles and reaches down for his bag.

DARK SUIT
(*dumps bag on table*)
My name's Cobb. Take a look for yourself.

The Young Man pauses, then, eyes on Cobb, he reaches forward and pulls the bag across the table. He unzips it and peers inside.

The Young Man looks puzzled. Cobb grins.

Inside the bag are CDs. Rummaging beneath them the Young Man uncovers some jewellery and a camera. He looks up at Cobb, puzzled.

COBB
(*smiling*)
What were you expecting, drugs?

YOUNG MAN

They're yours?

COBB
(*laughing*)

They are now.

YOUNG MAN
Why would you take their old CDs?

COBB

Easy to grab a load, easy to sell, totally untraceable. A good staple. The other stuff's more tricky, more unpredictable.

YOUNG MAN

You don't look like a burglar.

COBB

Sounds like a compliment.

The Young Man shrugs and smiles, zipping up the bag.

(*grinning broadly*)

Interested now?

FADE TO BLACK.

EXT. ENTRANCE TO BASEMENT BAR/CLUB – DUSK

The Blonde approaches, pauses, looking behind herself as if suspicious of being followed. She goes down the stairs into the club.

The Young Man (short hair, clean-shaven) approaches the entrance, pauses, uncertain. He looks about, then dives in.

INT. BASEMENT BAR/CLUB – DUSK

Three-sided bar, booths and tables, music.

The Young Man enters. The place is not full. The Blonde is seated at the bar. She watches the Young Man come in, then looks away, uninterested.

The Young Man approaches the bar, leaning on it several places along from The Blonde, glancing at her out of the corner of his eye. She is oblivious to his presence, as is the bartender, who is on the phone behind the bar. The Young Man sneaks looks at The Blonde whilst tapping the bar, waiting for the bartender to hang up the phone. The Blonde has an elegant profile, as seen from along the bar, but she looks unhappy.

The bartender hangs up the phone, shuffles over and looks enquiringly at the Young Man.

YOUNG MAN

Beer.

The bartender grabs a bottle from the fridge, opens it and sets it down in front of the Young Man. The bartender holds up a glass and raises his eyebrows at the Young Man, who shakes his head and raises the bottle to his lips, taking a sip. The Young Man puts the bottle back on the bar and turns to look at The Blonde. He gets off his barstool and moves down towards her, sliding his beer along the bar as he goes. He stops at her side.

Buy you a drink?

THE BLONDE
(*staring ahead*)
Yeah, but you can't sleep with me.

The Young Man smiles quizzically.

YOUNG MAN
Why not?

The Blonde turns to look at him, a movement of the head, nothing else, her expression hard to read.

THE BLONDE
I'm with him.

She jerks her head behind them. The Young Man turns, seeing three men seated at a table across the room, papers on the table, apparently talking business. Suits, ties, two of them young, one middle-aged and bald.

YOUNG MAN
(*turning back*)
Not that bald one?

THE BLONDE
He'll let you buy me a drink, but sex is out of the question.

YOUNG MAN
I see.

THE BLONDE
Still want to buy me that drink?

YOUNG MAN
No.

Right answer; The Blonde laughs. The Young Man sips from his beer.

So what's a beautiful young woman like you doing –

THE BLONDE

In a place like this?

YOUNG MAN

– with a bald old cunt like that?

THE BLONDE

Long story. Keep your voice down, he owns this place.

YOUNG MAN

Just trying to get your attention. You're interested now, aren't
you?

THE BLONDE
(*turning away*)

No.

*The Young Man is disarmed. He looks at the label of his beer for some-
thing to say.*

YOUNG MAN

I'm Timothy Kerr – Tim to my friends.

THE BLONDE
(*without looking at him*)

So?

*The Young Man opens his mouth, pissed off, but changes his mind
before he speaks.*

YOUNG MAN
(*softly*)

You've obviously had a bad day, one of those days which
makes you feel that everybody's out for their pound of
flesh.

The Blonde turns to look at him, her expression softer, but not much.

THE BLONDE
(*slow, considered delivery*)
That is the kind of day I've been having lately.

She glances out of the corner of her eye towards Baldy. He is watching them.

>   (*looking back to Young Man*)
Say something to me.

>   YOUNG MAN
Such as?

The Blonde slaps the Young Man hard across the face. He looks shocked.

>   THE BLONDE
>   (*turning to her drink*)
I'll be outside in ten minutes.

EXT. ENTRANCE TO BASEMENT BAR/CLUB – NIGHT

The Young Man is loitering outside.

The Blonde comes up out of the club and walks towards the Young Man without appearing even to notice him. He falls into step beside her. They don't speak for several paces.

>   THE BLONDE
Live close?

>   YOUNG MAN
Yeah. You live, I mean, you, do you live around here?

>   THE BLONDE
I do. But I don't want to go back there.

>   YOUNG MAN
Because of the bald guy.

>   THE BLONDE
No.

>   YOUNG MAN
You want to go to my place?

>   THE BLONDE
>   (*laughing*)
Don't get your hopes up. I can't be seen with you in any of

the bars around here. Got anything to drink at home?

YOUNG MAN

We can stop on the way.

FADE TO BLACK.

INT. CAFÉ — DAY

The Young Man sits alone at a table by the window, watching the building opposite. He has short hair and wears sunglasses to hide the worst of his facial bruises, but his swollen lip is still noticeable.

In front of him on the table are a cup of coffee, a notebook and a pen. He sips at the coffee.

EXT. OFFICE BUILDING — DAY

Young Man's POV from the café. Baldy exits the building and hails a taxi.

INT. CAFÉ — DAY

The Young Man opens the notebook and writes in it, and we:

FADE TO BLACK.

INT. OUTSIDE THE DOOR TO A FLAT, THE LANDING OF A NARROW STAIRWAY — DAY

Cobb comes up the stairs and stops outside the door.

The Young Man (he has long hair and is unshaven) follows, standing behind Cobb, looking over Cobb's shoulder as he examines the door.

Cobb knocks gingerly on the door. After a pause he reaches into his jacket pocket and pulls out a pair of rubber surgical gloves. He inflates the gloves one after the other before putting them on, interlacing his fingers and bumping the gloves snugly into place. He turns to the Young Man.

COBB
(whispering)

Gloves?

The Young Man nods and holds up his hands for inspection – he is wearing thick leather and wool gloves.

Cobb rolls his eyes. Shaking his head, he turns back to the door, then pushes the Young Man back and lifts up the doormat. There's nothing under there, and he lets it back down. The Young Man leans forward to whisper into Cobb's ear.

> YOUNG MAN
> (*whispering*)
> People don't really do that, do they?

> COBB
> (*whispering, reaching into his pocket*)
> You'd be surprised.

He takes a piece of plastic out and starts working it into the crack between the door and the frame.

The Young Man notices a potted plant on the windowsill. He reaches over and shifts it slightly, finding a key underneath it. He taps Cobb on the shoulder and, when he turns around, the Young Man holds it up in front of his face. Cobb smiles as he grabs it, and turns back to the door to unlock it.

> (*whispering*)
> Beginner's luck.

Cobb opens the door and heads inside, the Young Man following.

INT. HALLWAY – DAY

No lights – cold grey daylight filtered through net curtains.

Cobb is first, creeping forward through the flat with the Young Man at his shoulder. Cobb looks left and right into doorways as they advance, gently pushing them open to see inside and to let more light into the hallway. At the end of the hall Cobb turns to face the Young Man.

> COBB
> (*speaking normally now*)
> See, nobody home. Right, first things first. We need a bag.

YOUNG MAN
(*whispering*)

A bag?

COBB

To carry the stuff out of here. Why are you whispering?

Cobb passes through a door off to the left.

INT. BEDROOM – DAY

*A futon, two wardrobes, piles of books and neatly folded clothes by the
wall. Cobb crosses the room to the first wardrobe and opens it, rummaging around the bottom.*

COBB
(*head in wardrobe*)

Bingo.

He backs out of the wardrobe clutching a soft overnight bag.

YOUNG MAN
(*not whispering, but still quiet*)

Don't you have your own?

COBB

Yeah, sure, it's a big bag with 'swag' written across the side.
OK . . . what do you fancy?

The Young Man looks around and shrugs.

Not much in here of any value.

YOUNG MAN

You don't seem too concerned.

COBB

I don't do it for the money.

YOUNG MAN

So why –

COBB

For the adrenalin. Because I'm interested in people.

The Young Man raises his eyebrows.

You can tell a lot about people from their stuff. How old would you say these people were?

The Young Man shrugs.

From the futon you can make a pretty good guess. Young people have futons. I'd be surprised if they were anywhere near forty with a futon. But they've got one laundry bag so they're very used to each other which makes me think that they're over twenty-five.

YOUNG MAN
But if they're only twenty they could have been living together for years.

COBB
Look at the books. They're educated – went to college, graduated when they were twenty-one or twenty-two, wouldn't have moved in with each other until at least the last year of college. Get a better idea from their music.

He starts to examine the shelves, running surgeon's fingers across the shelves, touching things without picking them up. He comes across a wooden box.

Here's the box.

YOUNG MAN
What box?

COBB
Everybody's got a box. With men it's usually a shoebox.

YOUNG MAN
With valuables inside?

COBB
No. More interesting, more personal. Letters, odd snapshots, a plastic toy out of a Christmas cracker, a pebble from some beach.

He opens the box. The Young Man looks over his shoulder.

(*picking through the contents*)
See? Photos, odd bits of paper, worthless plastic jewellery. An unconscious collection. A display.

YOUNG MAN

Display?

COBB

Yes, a display. Each object showing something about the person, together adding up to an illustration of their personality. We've all got something of the artist inside of us, even if it is unconscious. It's extremely personal. We're privileged to see it. People rarely show anyone their box.

Cobb stares lovingly at the contents of the box for a few seconds before suddenly throwing it across the room, spilling the contents everywhere with surprising violence.

YOUNG MAN
(*taken aback*)

Why'd you do that?

COBB
(*extremely intense*)

It's like a diary. They hide it, but secretly they want someone to look at it and that's what I do. Concealment, display; flip sides of the same coin. This way they know that someone's seen it. That's what it's all about, interrupting someone's life, making them think about all the things they usually take for granted. That's what you're doing when you steal their things. When they collect the insurance money they go out to buy all these things that have just been sitting on their shelves, stuff they'd forgotten they'd bought, and they have to think all over again about why they wanted this stuff, what it's for. You take it away and show them what they had.

He moves to the laundry bag and reaches into his pocket. He pulls out a pair of lace panties, holding them up for the Young Man to see.

Saucy, eh? I took them from the last place, two young women sharing a flat.

The Young Man looks totally baffled as Cobb reaches into the laundry

24

*bag and pulls out a pair of trousers. He stuffs the panties into the front
left pocket and sticks the trousers back into the bag. He heads towards
the door, passing the baffled Young Man.*

(*winking*)
Give 'em something to chat about.

Cobb leaves the bedroom. The Young Man follows.

INT. HALLWAY — DAY

*Cobb walks down the corridor carrying the bag, the Young Man behind
him.*

YOUNG MAN
Why did you do that?

COBB
(*over his shoulder*)
She'll find them in his trousers and want to know what he's
been up to.

YOUNG MAN
Why would you want to fuck up their relationship?

*Cobb spins about to face the Young Man so abruptly that they almost
collide. There is a manic, intense look in his eyes.*

COBB
(*deadly serious*)
Don't you listen? You take it away and show them what they
had.

*The Young Man is speechless. Cobb turns and from in front of him we
can see a mischievous grin break across his face which is hidden from
the Young Man. Cobb dives through a doorway. The Young Man
shakes his head and heads after him.*

INT. KITCHEN — DAY

*Cobb is taking two glasses down from the cupboard. There is a bottle of
red wine on the counter.*

The Young Man enters.

25

COBB

Fancy a drink?

The Young Man looks at the bottle then at Cobb.

YOUNG MAN

You've got to be joking.

COBB
(*rummaging in a drawer*)
Don't be fooled by the supermarket label – it's quite good,
I've had it before.

*He takes a corkscrew out of the drawer and starts to open the bottle, his
hands smooth and graceful – surgical, almost – in their white latex
sheaths.*

(*levering the cork out*)
You'd have trouble doing this with *your* gloves on.

*He places the corkscrew on the counter and pours two glasses of wine,
handing one to the Young Man, who sips at it. Cobb picks up the
corkscrew and starts to remove the cork from it.*

YOUNG MAN

So are we going to take anything?

COBB
(*placing the corkscrew back into the drawer*)
Anything your heart desires. But look, that's not the point,
that's just work. *This* is what it's all about – being here.
Entering someone's life, finding out who they are . . . just feel
it – standing in someone's kitchen, drinking their wine,
someone you'll never even meet.

He jams the cork into the neck of the bottle and sticks it up on the shelf.

*Just as he does so there is the unmistakable sound of the front door
being opened.*

*Cobb spins around to face the kitchen door. The Young Man throws his
glass down on to the counter.*

We hear a muffled voice through the door.

26

WOMAN (O.S.)
Drink? I've got some wine.

MAN (O.S.)
Why not?

Cobb stands frozen, tense, staring at the door. The Young Man looks terrified, glancing from the back of Cobb's head to the door and back.

YOUNG MAN
(*tense whisper*)
What the fuck do –

COBB
(*hissing*)
SHHHHH!

The door swings open and Cobb's face transforms into an expression of innocent surprise. A young Woman stands frozen in the doorway, shocked. Cobb steps forward, palms open.

(*friendly, relaxed*)
You startled us! From the agency or viewing, like us?

As he speaks he has moved right up to the Woman, coming close enough that she feels compelled to step back into the hall. The Young Man follows, still looking nervous, but the Woman's attention is on Cobb.

WOMAN
(*tense, confused*)
What are you doing in my flat?

INT. HALLWAY – DAY

The Woman comes into the hall followed by the Young Man. Cobb turns his attention to the older man, who stands frozen in the hall, looking as nervous as the Young Man.

COBB
(*to the Woman*)
Viewing it. The agent said you'd be out this afternoon.

                              WOMAN
                           (*bewildered*)
But we're not moving.

                               COBB
                  (*to older man, ignoring Woman*)
You must be the man of the house. You have a lovely home.

*The older man looks nervously to the Woman. The Young Man and
Cobb are both now at the door.*

We'll leave you in peace, then.

                              WOMAN
But we're not moving!

                               COBB
                  (*opening door, looks bewildered*)
Not even at the end of the month?

                              WOMAN
NO!

The Woman notices their gloves.

Cobb notices her noticing.

                               COBB
               (*motioning the Young Man out the door*)
I should check with the agent, then, luv. Sorry to have both-
ered you.

He leaves, closing the door in the couple's bewildered faces.

EXT. ROOFTOP – DAY

*The Young Man comes out of a doorway on to the flat roof, hurrying,
followed by Cobb. Cobb closes the door behind him.*

                               COBB
Shouldn't have come back up here. We'll have to wait ages
before we go down. Maybe there's another way off here.

He starts to look around the edges of the roof.

28

YOUNG MAN

Jesus shit. You think they believed you?

COBB

(*laughing*)

Of course they didn't fucking believe me!

YOUNG MAN

So what did –

COBB

I just confused them. We caught them on the hop.

YOUNG MAN

How do you mean?

COBB

That bloke wasn't the boyfriend. Why do you think he didn't say anything? They were up to no good and she was probably glad that we weren't her boyfriend.

YOUNG MAN

You reckon?

COBB

Definitely. Why else would she be home from work in the middle of the afternoon? You just can't plan for that kind of shit. We were unlucky. Don't be put off. It's not going to happen next time.

YOUNG MAN

I'm not so sure.

COBB

(*offended*)

Oh yeah? Well next time you can do the prep work.

YOUNG MAN

I didn't mean that –

COBB

I'm serious. You pick a mark, check it out to your own satis-faction – days, months, years, whatever – and that's what we'll hit next.

YOUNG MAN
(*thoughtfully*)

Yeah. Yeah, all right.

COBB

Tell you what.

YOUNG MAN

What?

COBB

I feel bad about pulling the panty routine on that bloke –
she'll give him a load of shit, and it's her that's screwing
around.

The Young Man laughs, releasing tension.

FADE TO BLACK.

INT. LIVING ROOM – NIGHT

*Small, eclectic mix of stuff. Rubber plant, portable TV, desk, portable
stereo. The Blonde circles the room slowly, looking at various items, her
overcoat still on.*

*The Young Man enters (he has short hair and is clean-shaven), carry-
ing two glasses.*

*The Blonde hasn't heard him come in. He watches her from the door-
way as she reaches out to touch a ceramic candlestick sitting on a
shoulder-high shelf. As she touches the candlestick it falls into two
pieces. As she grabs at them she notices the Young Man watching her.*

THE BLONDE
(*flustered*)

I'm sorry, I just touched it, it –

YOUNG MAN

Just came apart in your hands.

THE BLONDE

No, really, it did.

The Young Man smiles as he moves into the room.

YOUNG MAN

I know, it was already broken. Somebody dropped it, I was going to glue it . . .

He grabs two pieces, putting the glasses down on the shelf in their place.

. . . but sod it, I'll never get around to it.

He drops the pieces into a waste-paper basket.

(*gesturing at chair*)

Take a seat.

The Blonde perches on the edge of a chair, her coat still on. The Young Man takes a bottle out of a plastic bag, opens it and pours two measures. He hands The Blonde a drink. She sips at it. She looks cold.

So what about the bald guy?

THE BLONDE

What about him?

YOUNG MAN

You're going out with him?

THE BLONDE

Not exactly.

YOUNG MAN

But you and him are –

THE BLONDE

(*matter-of-factly*)

I used to have a thing going with him, but it's been over for a long time.

YOUNG MAN

So why did you tell me you were with him?

THE BLONDE

To get rid of you.

YOUNG MAN

(*grins*)

So when you decided to have a drink with me, why did we have to come here?

THE BLONDE

He still gets jealous, he's a dangerous person. And I don't want to go to my place right now.

YOUNG MAN
(*probing*)

Why not?

THE BLONDE

I was burgled yesterday.

YOUNG MAN

Really? What did it feel like, to find your place broken into?

THE BLONDE

That's an odd question. Most people ask 'What did they take?'

YOUNG MAN

I'm curious about the way people feel about things.

He moves to the desk, reaching at a black case which sits amidst the papers and assorted crap.

I'm a writer.
(*opening the case to reveal an ancient manual typewriter*)
See?

THE BLONDE
(*deadpan*)

Gosh.

YOUNG MAN

So?

THE BLONDE

So?

YOUNG MAN

How did it feel?

THE BLONDE
(*annoyed*)

Great. How do you *think* it felt? I don't really want to talk about it, thank you.

The Young Man shrugs.

> YOUNG MAN

Sorry.

He straddles the chair which is in front of the desk. He leans in towards The Blonde.

So the bald guy's dangerous?

> THE BLONDE
> (*laughing*)

Christ, you're a nosy bastard.

> YOUNG MAN

Dangerous like how?

> THE BLONDE

Dangerous like criminal type, involved with bad things type dangerous.

> YOUNG MAN

What sort of bad things?

> THE BLONDE

The usual: girls, drugs, magazines.

> YOUNG MAN

Magazines?

> THE BLONDE

And films . . . pornography. And he owns a couple of clubs.

> YOUNG MAN

Wealthy?

> THE BLONDE

Yes. And refined. It took me a long time to realize the sort of things which he was capable of.

> YOUNG MAN

What sort of things?

> THE BLONDE

Perhaps another time. I think I'd better be going.

FADE TO BLACK.

INT. LIVING ROOM — DAY

The Young Man stands at the window, watching people pass by on the street below. He has short hair and his face is badly bruised.

He picks up the telephone and dials a number. After a few rings the phone is answered by a man we might recognize as Cobb.

> COBB (O.S.)
>
> Yeah?

> YOUNG MAN
>
> It's me . . . Bill.

> COBB (O.S.)
>
> What the fuck do you want?

> YOUNG MAN
>
> Advice.

A pause.

> COBB (O.S.)
>
> On what?

> YOUNG MAN
>
> The job.

> COBB (O.S.)
>
> What fucking job?

> YOUNG MAN
>
> The one I asked you about.

> COBB (O.S.)
>
> Not interested.

> YOUNG MAN
> (*snorting*)
>
> I gathered that. I'm doing it on my own. I wondered about protection.

> COBB (O.S.)
>
> Protection?

YOUNG MAN

Self-defence, weapon of some sort. Surprisingly enough, I thought you might be able to advise.

Cobb laughs at the other end of the phone.

COBB (O.S.)

Steel whip, nun-chucks – they're all right. Tools are good: sharpened screwdriver, hammer, chisel –

YOUNG MAN

Hammer?

COBB (O.S.)

Yeah, medium size, good rubber grip – very nasty. Get a claw hammer you can pry doors with it. Slip it into the back of your waistband, you're set.

The Young Man's eyes have glazed over – he doesn't seem to be listening.

You still there?

The Young Man hangs up without a word, and we:

FADE TO BLACK.

EXT. OUTSIDE THE DOOR TO A FLAT – DAY

Cobb and the Young Man (he has long hair and is unshaven) are putting on their gloves.

Cobb looks at the Young Man's leather gloves.

COBB

Why don't you get some of these, for Christ's sake?

YOUNG MAN

Where do you get them?

COBB

Stole a box from the Middlesex Hospital, but you can buy them.

He bends down and checks under the doormat. He straightens up, holding a key.

Bing-fucking-go.

He unlocks the door and they step cautiously inside.

INT. DIMLY LIT HALLWAY OF THE FLAT — DAY

Cobb proceeds slowly down the hall, pushing open each interior door and checking the various rooms. He stops at the last door.

> COBB
>
> You find a bag, I'll check out the stuff.

INT. LIVING ROOM — DAY

A small room with an eclectic mix of stuff; rubber plant, portable TV, desk, portable stereo.

Cobb enters and circles around the room, running his gloved hands across the mantelpiece, rubber-plant leaves, etc.

The Young Man enters, carrying a sports bag.

> YOUNG MAN
>
> Here we go.

> COBB
> *(almost to himself)*
> That was quick. We may not need it . . .
> *(he looks at the Young Man)*
> . . . there's fuck-all here.

Tight on the Young Man's face; he's really interested.

> YOUNG MAN
>
> Oh?

> COBB
> *(sarcastic)*
> Oh.

The Young Man looks around. Cobb prowls around the room danger-ously.

> YOUNG MAN
>
> What about the stereo?

Cobb has stopped at some shelves. Near his shoulder is a ceramic candlestick, no candle in it.

                              COBB
How much would *you* pay for a second-hand, ten-year-old
portable stereo? You want to carry it, you can have it. This is
fucking useless.

*He tips the candlestick off the shelf and on to the floor. It breaks in two
when it hits the floor.*

                          YOUNG MAN
                          (*surprised*)
Hey, what are we – vandals or burglars?

                              COBB
You're a burglar? So burgle.

                          YOUNG MAN
Well . . . what about the CDs?

Cobb crosses to the small CD rack.

                              COBB
                         (*interested now*)
Not much of a collection.

                          YOUNG MAN
                        (*drawing him out*)
Oh?

                              COBB
                       (*flipping through CDs*)
Very little here. And what there is seems quite personal.

                          YOUNG MAN
How's that?

                              COBB
There's none of the music that people play when their
friends come round, you know, not to be listened to or even
noticed but to fill the gaps in conversation.

                          YOUNG MAN
Like what?

                               37

COBB
(*glances around room*)
For someone this age . . . I dunno, maybe Simply Red or
Fleetwood Mac, that sort of shit.

YOUNG MAN
He's got good taste?

Cobb moves over to the desk.

COBB
Each to his own. But he's a sad fucker with no social life.

*The Young Man raises his eyebrows. At the desk Cobb flips open a
black case to reveal an ancient typewriter.*

Nice machine.

YOUNG MAN
You think *he's* a writer?

COBB
(*scoffing*)
If he wanted to write he'd have a word processor. He doesn't
want to write, he wants to be a writer – and that's two . . .
(*noticing something*)
. . . two completely different things.
(*turns to Young Man*)
You checked this out, right?

YOUNG MAN
Right.

COBB
(*suspicious*)
You watched him come and go, saw his routine?

YOUNG MAN
(*defensive*)
I told you, I checked it out. Why?

Cobb turns to the desk and stares at it, hard.

COBB
This guy's unemployed.

YOUNG MAN

No he isn't.

COBB
(*emphatic*)
He's unemployed. Look at this desk, people with jobs don't
want this shit in their living rooms!
(*rummaging through papers, files*)
This guy is unemployed or a student . . . either way he could
be back any fucking second!

YOUNG MAN
(*concerned*)
He won't. I watched him come and go, he's got a job.

COBB
(*rummaging*)
Yeah? What's he do, then?

YOUNG MAN
(*insistent*)

I checked it out.

Cobb stops rummaging, turns around and glares at the Young Man.

COBB
(*malevolent*)
What the fuck is this, then?

He holds up a booklet.

(*controlled anger*)
You should recognize this, Dole-boy . . .
(*steps forward*)
. . . his fucking UB40.

He grabs the Young Man and throws him against the wall.

*He holds the Young Man's face with his left hand and slaps the booklet
across it with the other, hard.*

Checked it out! You fucking arsehole, are you trying to get us
thrown in jail? We're leaving now.

He releases the Young Man, staring at him for a few seconds before

39

walking out of the living room. The Young Man rubs his face before
following.

INT. HALL — DAY

The Young Man hurtles after Cobb, who is almost at the front door.

> YOUNG MAN
> Aren't we going to take anything?

> COBB
> We're going now. I don't steal from no-hope dole scroungers.
> No offence.

> YOUNG MAN
> (*to himself*)
> None taken.

Cobb opens the front door and turns to face the approaching Young Man.

> COBB
> There's another place. One that *I've* checked out . . .

They leave, closing the door behind them.

FADE TO BLACK.

EXT. ROW OF TERRACED TOWNHOUSES — DAY

*The Young Man (with short hair and clean-shaven) loiters at the bus
stop, watching The Blonde's second-floor windows. The curtains are
pulled back to reveal The Blonde. She stands at the window. The front
door opens and Baldy steps out.*

*The Young Man watches Baldy as he walks down the steps on to the
street and turns right, away from the Young Man.*

*The Young Man waits for a few seconds before walking up to the front
door and ringing The Blonde's buzzer. The front door clicks unlocked
and the Young Man heads inside.*

INT. HALLWAY OUTSIDE THE BLONDE'S FLAT — DAY

*The Young Man comes up to the door and knocks; the door pushes open
slightly with the force of the knock.*

THE BLONDE (O.S.)
(*from within*)

It's open!

The Young Man enters.

INT. HALL OF A LARGE APARTMENT — DAY

Noise of a shower running, steam coming out of an open doorway.

The Young Man comes down the hall, cautiously. The Blonde comes out of a doorway in a bathrobe, glances at him.

THE BLONDE

You're early.

She disappears into the bathroom before the Young Man has a chance to reply.

THE BLONDE (O.S)

Make yourself at home, I'll be a minute.

The Young Man comes down the corridor. As he comes past the bathroom he sees that she has only half-closed the door – he peers in, but sees only a towel rail and steam. He goes through the next doorway along.

INT. LIVING ROOM — DAY

Expensively and tastefully decorated, almost cluttered – some pictures on the walls, lots of plants.

The Young Man comes into the room, glances around. He moves over to a small table by the wall and looks down at it. There is nothing on it. He runs his fingers over the polished wood surface, then turns around, looking about the room for something that he can't find. He crosses the room and sits down in a large armchair near the windows.

The Blonde enters, still in her robe, rubbing her wet hair with a towel.

YOUNG MAN

Nice place.

THE BLONDE
(*sitting down on the couch*)
Thanks. I can't stand the idea that some stranger was in
here, rummaging around. Creepy.

YOUNG MAN
What'd they take?

THE BLONDE
CD player, CDs, stuff like that. They took one of my bags to
carry it in – the police told me that that's pretty standard.

YOUNG MAN
Must be bad – losing that stuff.

THE BLONDE
(*shrugging*)
Insurance'll cover it. The personal stuff was worse.

YOUNG MAN
Personal stuff?

THE BLONDE
They took some of my things. They rifled through my underwear.

YOUNG MAN
Probably thought you kept valuables hidden there.

THE BLONDE
(*shaking her head with evident distaste*)
They took some of it.

YOUNG MAN
Shit. Why would they do that?

THE BLONDE
(*mocking*)
Come on, don't play the innocent, you're a man – you know
the sort of kinky voyeuristic shit men get up to.

YOUNG MAN
(*shaking his head*)
No. No, no, no . . . I'm not into that kind of . . .

THE BLONDE

So you have no interest in women's underwear whatsoever?

YOUNG MAN

No. I'm interested in what's inside it, that's all.

THE BLONDE

So if I offered you a pair of my panties, you wouldn't be
remotely interested?

YOUNG MAN

'Fraid not, though I'm sure they're lovely. Now you've
embarrassed me enough, thanks.

THE BLONDE
(*shrugging*)

Well, *they* took some. I'll tell you what else, they took one of
my earrings – not the pair, just *one* of the earrings. Bloody
annoying.

YOUNG MAN

Maybe you've just misplaced it.

THE BLONDE

No. I know where it was – they took it . . . just to fuck me
around. Bloody annoying, they probably think they're really
clever. I wear the one they left on its own.

YOUNG MAN

Why?

THE BLONDE
(*shrugs*)

Makes me feel good and miserable. I don't know, gives me
something to talk about, anyway.

She sighs and looks over to the window.

(*rising*)
Give me a minute, I'll get dressed.

*She leaves. As soon as she is out of the room the Young Man jumps out
of his chair and lifts up the seat cushion, looking underneath. He
thrusts his hands down the back and sides of the chair, feeling for some-*

43

thing. He comes up empty-handed, puzzlement on his face, and replaces the cushion.

He goes into the hall and crosses to another doorway.

INT. HALLWAY — DAY

The Young Man pauses at the door. It is open a crack and through the crack he can see into the bedroom.

INT. BEDROOM — DAY

The Young Man's POV through the crack shows us The Blonde almost dressed, buttoning her blouse in front of the mirror.

The Young Man watches for a second or two, then pushes the door open quietly.

The Blonde turns her head to look at him, apparently unsurprised. The Young Man moves towards her. She allows him to reach out and pull her towards him. He kisses her on the lips and we:

FADE TO BLACK.

EXT. OFFICE BUILDING IN SOHO — DAY

The Young Man loiters outside. He has short hair and wears dark glasses. Baldy exits with another man. They hail a cab and leave.

The Young Man wanders down an alley running down the side of the building. He takes a piece of paper out of his pocket on which a rough floor plan has been drawn.

He counts windows down the side of the building, stopping at a particular window to study it. He looks around, puts the paper back into his pocket and walks back out on to the main street.

INT. BEDROOM — DAY

Small, dark, cluttered.

The Young Man enters, carrying a paper bag. He removes his sunglasses, revealing his bruised face.

He tosses the paper bag on to the bed, then reaches into the breast

44

pocket of his suit jacket and pulls out a pair of rubber surgical gloves.

He inflates one before stretching it on to his fingers, then does the same with the second, interlacing his fingers to jam the gloves on snugly. He flexes his hands, then turns to the bed and reaches into the paper bag, removing a brand new hammer with a rubber grip and a claw head.

He tests the weight of the hammer, first in one hand then in the other. He awkwardly sticks the hammer into the back of his waistband and moves to the dusty mirror, examining himself. He removes the hammer from his waistband and looks at himself holding it in the mirror, and we:

FADE TO BLACK.

INT. INSIDE THE HALL OF A LARGE APARTMENT — DAY

Little is visible in the gloom. All is quiet.

Suddenly a splintering crash breaks the silence and the front door breaks inward, revealing Cobb and the Young Man (long hair, unshaven), gloves on, glancing about nervously.

Cautiously, they creep into the flat. Cobb shuts the door behind them. The Young Man moves to the nearest doorway and opens the door, spilling a cold, diffuse light into the hall. He opens the next door along and looks in and we

CUT TO:

INT. LIVING ROOM — DAY

Young Man's POV: expensively and tastefully decorated, almost cluttered – lots of pictures on the walls, lots of plants.

The Young Man steps back into the hall.

INT. HALL — DAY

The Young Man looks over at Cobb.

> YOUNG MAN
> (*whispering loudly*)

Not bad at all.

Cobb turns to look at him.

COBB
(*speaking normally*)

I'll check the bedroom for a bag, you check out the stuff.

The Young Man nods and passes into the living room.

INT. LIVING ROOM – DAY

The Young Man enters and crosses to the centre of the large room. He turns around, scanning the room, taking in furniture, stereo, plants, TV and VCR, pictures.

Noticing something, he moves closer to a group of pictures on the wall.

He leans in to study them and his POV reveals a collection of framed photographs of the same young woman. In some of them she is obviously posed; the black-and-white ones in particular look like professionally shot modelling photos. The young woman is an attractive blonde.

He stares at the pictures for a few seconds, then turns back to the room. He crosses to the small table with some framed photographs on it and leans over to examine the pictures. They are all of The Blonde. The Young Man picks up one of the framed photos and looks at it more closely.

COBB (O.S.)

Hey! Take a look in here!

The Young Man places the picture back on the table, keeping his eyes on it until he has moved several steps towards the door.

INT. HALL – DAY

The Young Man exits the living room and walks down the corridor looking into the rooms for Cobb. He enters a room near the front door.

INT. BEDROOM – DAY

Double bed, light, feminine, patterned fabrics and many cushions, a chest of drawers beneath a framed photograph.

Cobb is standing in front of the chest of drawers, the top drawer open.

46

He is holding up a garter belt for the Young Man to see.

COBB
(*mischievous, conspiratorial*)
Saucy lady, *n'est-ce que pas?*

The Young Man approaches, looking at the photograph above the chest of drawers – it is The Blonde looking serious.

Cobb turns to the chest of drawers and rummages around.

I haven't found a bag, yet.

The Young Man comes up beside Cobb and looks into the drawer – it is full of silk panties. Cobb rummages through them. He looks more interested in the panties themselves than anything he might find in them.

YOUNG MAN
This is her flat?

COBB
Yeah, and she's a fox.

YOUNG MAN
But she's got pictures of herself everywhere.

COBB
Yeah, and she looks good. Check this lot out.

He nods his head at the underwear. The Young Man hesitates and Cobb jerks his head again. The Young Man reaches into the drawer and feels through some of the silk undergarments. Cobb grabs a handful, puts them to his nose and inhales deeply, looking at the Young Man, who shakes his head and smiles pityingly. They stand there, two piggies at the trough. The Young Man grabs some of the panties and lifts them up. He glances up and freezes, seeing the picture of The Blonde looking down at him.

You should take some.

YOUNG MAN
What?! No way.

47

COBB
(*shrugs*)
Suit yourself. I'm going to, she's a babe.

He stuffs a handful of silk into his pocket and moves away from the chest of drawers. The Young Man glances at Cobb, then swiftly pockets some panties when Cobb has turned his back. The Young Man stares up at the picture of The Blonde as he backs away.

COBB (O.S.)
Bingo.

The Young Man turns to see Cobb displaying a large leather holdall. Cobb turns and points at a pair of pearl earrings on the dresser. He picks just one of them up and heads into the hall.

INT. LIVING ROOM – DAY

The Young Man is stuffing CDs into the leather holdall.

Cobb is slumped in a large armchair, watching.

The Young Man straightens up.

COBB
You should take that CD player. It's small enough.

The Young Man grabs the player, pulls wires out of the back and sticks it into the holdall. He moves over to a small desk. On the desk lies a set of passport photographs. He stares at four near-identical images of The Blonde.

YOUNG MAN
(*without turning round*)
Why does she have so many pictures of herself?

Cobb looks around the room.

COBB
I think she's a model. Certainly vain.

The Young Man slips the passport photos off the desk and into his pocket. Cobb notices but he doesn't say anything – just smiles to himself. The Young Man turns around. He avoids making eye contact with Cobb.

48

That about it?

Cobb looks lazily over the room

COBB

I think that covers the useful stuff.

He hauls himself out of his comfortable chair with a groan.

Let's go.

He holds up the single pearl earring.

(*mischievous*)
I'll just misplace this for her.

He pulls the seat cushion off the armchair, places the earring on the chair, dead centre, and replaces the cushion.

EXT. ROW OF TERRACED TOWNHOUSES — DAY

Cobb and the Young Man exit one of the front doors, the Young Man carrying a full leather holdall.

They turn down the road and walk briskly away.

INT. CHARING CROSS STATION LEFT-LUGGAGE OFFICE — DAY

The Young Man hands over the leather holdall, takes a ticket and offers it to Cobb.

COBB
(*refusing the ticket*)
It was your job. You hang on to the stuff.

They walk out of the station.

EXT. CHARING CROSS STATION — DAY

Cobb and the Young Man talk as they stroll away from the building.

COBB
Pick it up tomorrow and hang on to it till I let you know we're ready to fence it.

YOUNG MAN

Right.

Cobb looks thoughtfully at the Young Man.

COBB
(*seductive, drawing him in further*)
Unless, of course, you want to sell it yourself and just give
me my half of what you get for it.

YOUNG MAN
Wouldn't know how to go about it.

COBB
Look, about being hard on you back at that first place: I won't
let anyone put me at risk, it's dangerous enough already.

They stop, unsure how to proceed.

An early supper, I think.

YOUNG MAN
Look, I really can't afford –

COBB
(*smiling*)

It's covered.

FADE TO BLACK.

INT. RESTAURANT – NIGHT

Formal, expensive, white linen, mirrors.

*The Young Man and The Blonde are seated at a table in one corner;
cosy, intimate. They are having coffee.*

THE BLONDE

How was your food?

YOUNG MAN
(*looking down*)

Fine.

THE BLONDE

So what is it?

YOUNG MAN

You chose this restaurant because you knew we wouldn't run into him here.

THE BLONDE

So?

YOUNG MAN

You said it was over between the two of you.

THE BLONDE

It is.

YOUNG MAN

Then why –

THE BLONDE

I also said that he's dangerous.

The Young Man looks at her imploringly.

(*pitying but impatient*)

Fine. An example. One night he came back to the flat – *my* flat – with a couple of the thugs who work for him. That meant trouble; right away I could tell something was going to happen. Then, a little later, this other man arrives . . .

DISSOLVE TO:

INT. THE BLONDE'S FLAT, FRONT HALL – DAY

A heavy-set man opens the door to a smaller man and motions him towards the living room.

THE BLONDE (V.O.)

. . . you don't need to know who he was or anything about him except that he had cheated them out of some of their money . . .

INT. THE BLONDE'S FLAT, LIVING ROOM – DAY

The Blonde sits in the armchair, smoking, nervous. Baldy and a heavy-set man welcome the smaller man into the room.

THE BLONDE (V.O.)

. . . just money, that's all.

The two heavy-set men grab the smaller man and force him to the ground, spreading his arms out before him, pinning his wrists to the floor, one of them kneeling on his back.

Baldy brings the hammer down on to a finger with tremendous force.

The Blonde gets up to leave. Baldy looks up at her, pointing at her with the hammer.

BALDY

Stay. Watch.

The Blonde stops at the door and turns around. Baldy starts smashing all of the smaller man's fingers in turn.

The Blonde closes her eyes and presses her face against the door frame as if she's trying to burrow her way out.

CUT TO:

INT. RESTAURANT — NIGHT

The Young Man listens intently.

THE BLONDE

He smashed all of his fingers . . . then he split his head open . . .

CUT TO:

INT. THE BLONDE'S LIVING ROOM — DAY

Baldy grunts as he brings the hammer down sharply.

Baldy stands up and drops the hammer. There is blood.

The Blonde is crying.

BALDY

Give me a fucking tea-towel or something.

CUT TO:

INT. RESTAURANT — NIGHT

The Young Man is speechless. The Blonde sips at her coffee before continuing.

> THE BLONDE

Dangerous enough for you?

> YOUNG MAN

Is it true?

> THE BLONDE

Yes.

> YOUNG MAN

Christ. You don't see him any more?

> THE BLONDE
> (*deadpan*)

After he messed up my rug like that?

> YOUNG MAN

That's not funny.

> THE BLONDE

I know.

They both sip their coffees. The Young Man looks thoughtfully at her.

> YOUNG MAN

So how did you meet him?

> THE BLONDE

Let's not talk about him –

> YOUNG MAN
> (*bitter*)

Did you *work* for him?

> THE BLONDE
> (*furious*)

That's none of your fucking business! You're sick. And a hypocrite. You loved hearing that story, you want to hear some more for your jollies . . . you're as bad as the freak who stole my pants . . .

(*rising from the table*)
. . . well, you can fuck off, you filthy little shit.

She throws her napkin down, upsetting her water glass, and strides away from the table. The Young Man grabs the glass, mopping at the spilt water with the napkin. He looks around to see if the other diners have noticed (they have). He catches the waiter's eye and scribbles in the air for the bill.

He takes out a credit card. He looks down at it, turning it over in his hands before laying it down on the table.

The name on the card is Timothy Kerr.

FADE TO BLACK.

EXT. OFFICE BUILDING – NIGHT

The Young Man (short hair, sunglasses) glances around before diving into the side alleyway.

He moves along the building, counting the windows as he goes.

Finding the right one, he pulls his hammer out and levers it open using the claw. Looking about, he lifts the window and hauls himself through.

INT. OFFICE – NIGHT

Big desk, filing cabinets, couple of chairs.

The Young Man slithers through the window and on to the floor behind the desk.

He gets on to his haunches and removes his sunglasses, putting them into his breast pocket. He looks around the office. It is well lit from the streetlights outside the windows.

The Young Man moves to the bookshelves and starts to remove books, stacking them on the floor quickly but quietly.

Halfway through the second shelf he uncovers a safe set into the wall.

Excited, hands trembling, he removes a piece of paper from his pocket. It has a series of numbers written on it. He spins the dial according to the numbers. He tries the door – it won't open. He tries the combination again, pulls the door and this time it swings open to reveal a large stack of money. The Young Man is shocked by the amount. Next to the money is an A4 envelope.

YOUNG MAN

Bingo.

He pulls the money and the envelope out of the safe, leaving it in a pile on the floor. He stands up and looks around.

(*under his breath*)

Bag.

He opens the desk drawers, looking in each one. He opens the closet, searching around, finding nothing.

Increasingly frantic now, the Young Man paces around the room, peering into every corner, looking behind every piece of furniture. At length he stops, exasperated.

(*loud whisper*)

FUCK!

He looks at the bundles of banknotes. He looks at the cluttered desk. There is a roll of masking tape on the desk. The Young Man steps over, grabs the tape and pulls off a long strip, breaking it with his teeth, and we:

FADE TO BLACK.

INT. FRENCH RESTAURANT — DUSK

Understated. Expensive; polished wooden floors, starched linen, well-dressed clientele. The Young Man and Cobb are seated at a table near the back of the place.

Cobb eats his food with small, graceful movements. In his dark suit and tie he fits right in, unlike the Young Man, who is shabbily dressed, unshaven, has long, greasy hair and looks ill at ease.

Cobb finishes chewing a large bite of his steak, sips from his glass of water, then dabs his lips gently with his napkin.

COBB

You're developing a taste for it.

The Young Man looks up from his food.

The violating, the voyeurism – it's definitely you.

YOUNG MAN

I think not.

COBB

I think *so*. And I think before long you'll develop a taste for the things you can do with the proceeds.

YOUNG MAN

Such as?

COBB
(gesturing around them)

This.

YOUNG MAN

You make all of your money that way.

COBB
(smiling)

Not all of it. You're going to pay for this.

YOUNG MAN

But I told you, I can't afford –

He is silenced by Cobb throwing a credit card on to the table.

COBB

It won't really be you, it'll be . . .
(he tilts his head to look at the card)
Timothy Kerr. But I thought I'd give you the pleasure of pretending to pay.

YOUNG MAN

But how –

Cobb tosses a pen on to the table next to the card.

COBB

Sign it.

YOUNG MAN
(*picking up the card*)

Sign it?

He looks at the card. He turns it over; there is no signature on the white strip. He looks up at Cobb.

COBB

Sign it in your own handwriting and you can use it for anything. I wouldn't use it for more than a day or two, just to be safe.

YOUNG MAN
(*a whisper*)

Christ.

The two men smile at each other. The Young Man reaches for the pen. He signs the back and pockets the card, shaking his head and laughing.

Don't you worry about being caught?

COBB

Why else would I do it? Besides, I'm not going to get caught.

YOUNG MAN

You've thought it all through.

COBB
(*raises wine glass*)

I've thought it all through.
(*pause*)
This is just the tip of the iceberg, I do things you wouldn't believe.

YOUNG MAN

Such as?

COBB

An example. Sometimes when I'm watching a place I'll see that the owners are about to go on holiday. I'll wait till they've gone, then move in for a week or so.

YOUNG MAN

You've got to be joking.

COBB

Happens a lot more often than you'd think.

YOUNG MAN

But how do you know how long they'll be gone for?

COBB

Almost always marked on the kitchen calendar.

YOUNG MAN
(*a whisper*)

Christ.

He takes a sip from his wine, then shovels a forkful of food into his mouth. He chews for a second then freezes, his eyes locked on something at the far end of the restaurant, behind Cobb.

(*through steak*)

Jesus fucking Christ!

Cobb narrows his eyes.

COBB

What's wrong?

YOUNG MAN
(*swallows hard*)

The woman, the woman from that first place, the one who came home, the, the, the one who saw me – us . . . she just walked in.

The Young Man's POV shows us the young woman from the first robbery and a man, whom we have not seen before, waiting to be seated.

COBB
(*calm, not turning round*)

Are you sure?

YOUNG MAN

Yes, I'm fucking sure!

COBB
(*impatient*)

Is she with the same bloke?

YOUNG MAN

No.

COBB

We're all right then.

YOUNG MAN

All right?! What if she sees us?!

COBB

If she sees us, she won't do anything. She's with her partner now and she won't want to have to explain how she found us at their flat when she was supposed to be at work.

YOUNG MAN

That's one hell of a chance to take!

COBB

(*fed up*)

Look, just calm down. What would she do anyway? All we stole was half a bottle of an indifferent red wine. Just relax, keep your head.

The Young Man looks at his plate, trying to stay calm.

YOUNG MAN

You mind if we skip dessert?

COBB

(*with disgust*)

Yes, I fucking mind.

INT. FRENCH RESTAURANT – NIGHT

Later.

Cobb is scraping up the last of his chocolate mousse. An almost untouched dessert sits in front of the Young Man, who repeatedly glances up past Cobb's head. The Young Man's POV shows us the young woman seated with her companion at the other end of the restaurant.

The young woman pushes her chair back from the table, stands up, places her napkin on her chair and heads towards Cobb and the Young Man's table. The Young Man looks terrified.

YOUNG MAN

She's coming this way.

Cobb looks up from his chocolate mousse. He nods at a door off to his left.

COBB

She's going to the loo, relax.

The Young Man can't take his eyes off the young woman as she approaches.

She comes near their table. As she turns to the left she notices the Young Man and looks at him for an instant with something which might be recognition. She carries on, passing through the doors to the lavatories.

YOUNG MAN
(*losing it*)

She fucking looked at me!

COBB

Yeah?

YOUNG MAN

Yeah! She fucking knows – we have to leave!

Cobb places his spoon back into his dish and looks up at the Young Man with an almost bored expression.

COBB
(*gesturing to the waiter*)

We'll leave – not that we have anything to worry about other than you making a twat of yourself.

EXT. FRENCH RESTAURANT – NIGHT

Cobb and the Young Man exit. Cobb suddenly turns on the Young Man as if he might hit him.

COBB
(*pointing at the Young Man's face*)

You know, I really hate it when I don't get to finish a good meal with a coffee.

The Young Man looks flabbergasted.

YOUNG MAN

But –

COBB
(*bitter*)

Just don't fucking say it!

He waves at a taxi.

INT. BACK OF TAXI – NIGHT

Cobb looks out of the window like a sullen child. The Young Man looks at him, thinking.

YOUNG MAN

Look, she recognized me, OK? She's had a second look at me. It makes me nervous.

Cobb turns to the Young Man.

COBB
(*calm*)

If you're worried about being recognized, why don't you do something about your appearance? Haircut, smart clothes, your own mother won't recognize you.

The Young Man looks down at himself, chastened.

(*grinning to himself*)

Just because you break into people's homes doesn't mean you have to *look* like a criminal.

FADE TO BLACK.

EXT. ROW OF TERRACED TOWNHOUSES – NIGHT

The Young Man (short hair, clean-shaven) buzzes The Blonde.

THE BLONDE
(*voice on tannoy*)

Fuck off.

YOUNG MAN

How do you know it's me? Could be your mother you just told to fuck off.

THE BLONDE
(*voice on tannoy*)
I meant it.

YOUNG MAN
Please, just let me in . . . I've come to apologize.

The lock clicks open and he steps inside.

INT. THE BLONDE'S FLAT, HALLWAY — NIGHT

The Young Man walks slowly down the corridor. Passing the bedroom he sees The Blonde sitting on the bed. He stands in the doorway.

INT. BEDROOM — NIGHT

Double bed, light, feminine, patterned fabrics and many cushions, a chest of drawers.

The Blonde sits on the bed, legs crossed, smoking a cigarette. The Young Man considers his opening line.

THE BLONDE
So apologize.

YOUNG MAN
I haven't been entirely honest with you.

The Blonde raises her eyebrows.

I'm writing about burglaries.

THE BLONDE
(*confused*)
What?

YOUNG MAN
I'm researching burglaries, I'm, I'm doing a piece about a guy I know who burgles people. That's why I've been asking you questions about your burglary.

THE BLONDE
Why didn't you just tell me?

YOUNG MAN

I didn't want to upset you. See, I've been breaking into
houses with him – that is, he's been breaking in and I've been
watching him. I mean, I haven't taken anything or . . . whatever, I just go along and watch, for my research.

THE BLONDE

Is that it?

YOUNG MAN

Yes.

THE BLONDE

What does that have to do with anything?

YOUNG MAN

Now I've been honest with you, I'd like you to return the
favour.

THE BLONDE

I have been honest with you.

YOUNG MAN

You're still seeing the bald guy.

THE BLONDE
(*flustered*)

How do –

YOUNG MAN

I was early the other day. I saw him leave. You said it was
over.

THE BLONDE
(*resigned*)

It is.

YOUNG MAN
(*quizzical*)

Then why?

THE BLONDE

He's blackmailing me.

YOUNG MAN
You said he's rich – why would . . .

THE BLONDE
(*bitter*)
Who said anything about money?

The Young Man sighs. He slides down the wall to sit in the doorway, his back against the frame. After a moment's thought he looks up at The Blonde.

YOUNG MAN
What's he blackmailing you with?

THE BLONDE
Photos.

YOUNG MAN
Of what?

THE BLONDE
Of *me*. And don't ask me anything else about them. You'd only want the details to fuel your seedy little fantasies. Let's just say that my mother wouldn't frame them for her sideboard.

YOUNG MAN
You've got me all wrong, you know.

THE BLONDE
Have I?

The Young Man nods. He thinks for a moment.

YOUNG MAN
So where does he keep them?

THE BLONDE
In his office. Why?

YOUNG MAN
Maybe I can get them back.

THE BLONDE
How?

64

YOUNG MAN

Break in and take them. I can get my friend to do it with me
– there must be valuable stuff in his office, right?

THE BLONDE

He sometimes has money in his safe.

YOUNG MAN
(*shaking his head*)

No, we can't get into a safe –

THE BLONDE

That's where the pictures are.

YOUNG MAN

What?

THE BLONDE

In a manilla envelope in his safe, negatives and eight-by-ten
prints.

YOUNG MAN

Then we can't –

THE BLONDE

I know the combination.

YOUNG MAN

How?

THE BLONDE

I've seen him open it a million times. I've always figured that
I might get a chance to lift the photos.

YOUNG MAN

Right, that's what we'll do then.

He gets up and moves on to the bed.

THE BLONDE

Nobody in their right mind would steal from him.

YOUNG MAN
(*putting his arms around her*)

If we don't get caught it won't make any difference who it

was we stole from – and we won't get caught.

He kisses The Blonde. She pulls away to speak.

THE BLONDE

Just promise me one thing. If you get the pictures you'll bring them to me without looking at them, without even opening the envelope?

YOUNG MAN

Of course.

THE BLONDE

I've got your word?

YOUNG MAN

You have my word.

They kiss again.

FADE TO BLACK.

INT. OFFICE – NIGHT

The Young Man (short hair, bruised face) has taken his jacket off and is frantically taping bundles of money to his arms and around his waist. He works in a frenzy, ripping masking tape with his teeth, grabbing bundles and slapping them against his stomach. He covers his arms and abdomen, but there's still a lot more money, so he undoes his trousers, pulls them off and frantically starts to tape bundles to his bare legs. His jacket, the manilla envelope and his hammer are sitting on the desk. He grabs a bundle and tapes it to his ankle. He straightens up, looks at the remaining money.

YOUNG MAN
(*whisper*)

Fuck it.

He takes the tape and passes it around his midriff, securing the bundles which he has already taped to his waist. As he is doing so the overhead light snaps on and the Young Man freezes.

One of Baldy's business companions is standing in the office doorway, a look of amazement on his face. Neither man moves. The Young Man

66

eyes the hammer on the desk, within easy reach. He grabs it as he launches himself at Baldy's man, trailing bank notes in the air behind him as he flies across the room, hammer raised.

The Young Man brings the hammer down across the other man's head in a nasty sideswipe. The man goes down and doesn't get up. The Young Man moves back to the desk, shocked. He clumsily puts his trousers on over the money, than looks over at the man on the floor as he grabs for his suit jacket. The man is not moving; there is blood on his head and on the floor.

The Young Man gets his jacket on, tears his eyes away from the prone man to realize that he has blood on his hands and now on his previously white shirt. He shudders as he jams the bloody hammer into his waistband, grabs the manilla envelope and heads for the window. A last glance at the prone man before climbing out of the window.

EXT. SIDE STREET – NIGHT

The Young Man practically falls out of the window and on to the ground. He struggles to his feet, weaving like a drunk, and heads away from the office window towards the main street, and we:

FADE TO BLACK.

INT. BATHROOM – DAY

Small, cold, dingy.

The Young Man stands in front of the mirror, examining his longish hair and attempt at a beard.

He picks up some nail scissors and starts to cut his hair.

INT. BEDROOM – DAY

Small, dark, cluttered.

The Young Man is knotting a tie in front of a dusty, cracked mirror. He is wearing a dark suit, old-fashioned and well-worn. His hair is dramatically shorter; a ragged near-crew cut.

He plays with his hair, looking at his reflection. He rubs his newly shaven chin.

Close on the mirror we see that the strip of passport photos of The Blonde are wedged into the bottom right-hand corner of the frame.

The Young Man's eye is caught by the photos and he picks them up, looking closely at them, a thoughtful expression on his face.

CUT TO:

INT. LIVING ROOM — DAY

Lighter. Neater, apart from the paper-covered desk.

The Young Man is on the phone, waiting for it to be picked up at the other end. We hear the click as it is answered.

> MALE VOICE (O.S.)
>
> Yeah?

> YOUNG MAN
>
> Cobb? Bill.

> MALE VOICE (O.S.)
>
> Hello, 'Bill'.

CUT TO:

INT. INDISTINCT SURROUNDINGS; A WINDOW COVERED BY A NET CURTAIN — DAY

Cobb is standing by the window on the phone. He wears a white shirt, unbuttoned.

> COBB
>
> What can I do for you?

> YOUNG MAN (O.S.)
>
> Nothing too important.

CUT TO:

INT. LIVING ROOM — DAY

> YOUNG MAN
>
> It's about the stuff.

COBB (O.S.)

What about it?

The Young Man's other hand comes into frame; he is holding the passport photos as well as some bunched-up silk.

YOUNG MAN
(*staring at the photos*)

I've met a guy – I won't go into details. I'll take care of it myself, as you suggested, and you'll get half. I can't promise to get as much as you would but I'd like to give it a go. How does that sound?

COBB (O.S.)

Sounds fine. Anything else?

YOUNG MAN

I took your advice.

COBB (O.S.)

What advice?

YOUNG MAN

My appearance. I cut my hair, and I'm all dressed up.

COBB (O.S.)

'With no place to go.'

CUT TO:

INT. BY THE WINDOW – DAY

COBB

You know I wasn't being entirely serious about that.

YOUNG MAN (O.S.)

It makes me feel better.

COBB

Safer, huh?

YOUNG MAN (O.S.)

Safer. I'll give you a call when I've got the money.

COBB

Right.

He hangs up. We go wider and see that he is leaning on the windowsill in what appears to be a bedroom. His shirt is completely untucked and unbuttoned.

FEMALE VOICE (O.S.)

What was all that about?

COBB

You.

Cobb's POV shows us The Blonde, lying in bed, under the sheets but apparently naked.

Your stuff, anyway.

He clambers up on to the bed to lean against the wall beside The Blonde.

He's going to deal with it himself.

The Blonde lays her arm across Cobb's stomach and looks up at him.

THE BLONDE

Meaning?

COBB

Meaning he took the bait and he's hooked. He's going to hang on to your stuff, pretend to sell it, give me some money. If you're lucky he might even give you most of it back. It's perfect, the photos worked. I've even got him to cut his hair and change his clothes.

THE BLONDE

So are you going to tell me where you hid my earring, now?

COBB

(grinning)

No. And I wouldn't hold your breath for the return of your underwear, either. He'll be far too embarrassed to admit to stealing your panties.

THE BLONDE

Shit. And did you have to break down my door? Couldn't you have pretended to find the spare key?

COBB
(*laughing*)

Couldn't. That would have been three spare keys in a row – even 'Bill' isn't going to buy that. When we went to his place it was embarrassing – right under the mat, just like I told him . . . pathetic. It was a new mat as well, and I swear, I seriously think that he went out and bought the mat just so he could put his key under it.

The Blonde laughs. Cobb laughs.

FADE TO BLACK.

INT. YOUNG MAN'S BEDROOM – DAY

The Young Man is knotting his tie in front of the mirror.

The Blonde is lying on the bed behind him.

THE BLONDE

What if he won't help?

YOUNG MAN

Then I'll do it on my own.

THE BLONDE

How long will you be?

YOUNG MAN

Couple of hours.

EXT. CHARING CROSS STATION LEFT-LUGGAGE OFFICE – DAY

The Young Man hands over his ticket and collects the leather holdall.

EXT. HUNGERFORD BRIDGE – DAY

The Young Man crosses south, carrying the leather holdall.

INT. HALLWAY IN A BLOCK OF FLATS — DAY

The Young Man knocks on a door.

The door is opened by Cobb.

> COBB
> You're late.
> (*noticing the holdall*)
> You said you'd fenced it.

He steps back to let the Young Man in.

INT. LIVING ROOM — DAY

Comfortable, tastefully furnished.

Cobb is sitting on the couch. The Young Man stands at the window.

> COBB
> It'll take me a few days to sell all of it.

> YOUNG MAN
> Whatever.

> COBB
> Something else on your mind?

The Young Man turns to face Cobb.

> YOUNG MAN
> I want to break into a place.

> COBB
> I've been scouting a couple –

> YOUNG MAN
> A particular place. For some photos.

> COBB
> Photos?

> YOUNG MAN
> Photos. For a friend.

> COBB
> What's the place?

YOUNG MAN

Office. In a safe, but we'll have the combination.

COBB

If it's for a friend, where's the money in it?

YOUNG MAN

There's money in the safe . . . probably.

COBB

Probably? Whose office?

YOUNG MAN

Club-owner, pornographer type.

COBB

Heavy?

YOUNG MAN

From the sound of it.

Cobb exhales. He stares hard at the Young Man.

COBB

What the fuck's going on?

YOUNG MAN

I'm seeing someone. They need my help.

Cobb stands up and walks over to the Young Man.

COBB

Who are you seeing?

The Young Man looks away.

(*loud*)

Who?! Who are you seeing?!

The Young Man looks into Cobb's eyes.

YOUNG MAN

The owner of that bag.

COBB
(*confused*)

What?

73

YOUNG MAN

The woman who owns the flat we hit – the one with the pictures of herself.

COBB
(*barely concealed rage*)
Tell me you're fucking joking.

YOUNG MAN
(*excited*)
Her pictures – I was curious, I followed her, got to know her. She's . . . she's . . . she's . . . we're in love.

COBB
You've slept with her?

YOUNG MAN
(*unaware of Cobb's growing rage*)
Yeah. She's fantastic, amazing. That's why I haven't sold her stuff, I mean, I thought that I might give it back to her but that would mean –

COBB
That would mean telling her that it was you who fucking robbed her! How shrewd – How, how, how prudent of you not to tell her that!

The Young Man is quiet, realizing he has misjudged the situation.

Nice hair, by the way. And a nice suit, shame about the bloodstains, though.

YOUNG MAN
(*looks down at himself*)
Bloodstains?

Cobb punches him in the face then belts him in the stomach. The Young Man doubles over, groaning.

COBB
I fucking warned you!

He smiles as he brings his elbows down hard into the Young Man's back. The Young Man grunts and staggers to the side, just keeping on his feet. Cobb pushes him back across the room and charges at him.

I won't let anyone put me at risk!

As he speaks, Cobb grabs the Young Man's face with one hand and punches him hard in the face several times.

The Young Man slips to the floor, dragging Cobb down with him. The two men scrabble around on the floor, the Young Man putting up a fight until Cobb finally swivels round and boots him in the ribs, then the face.

The Young Man groans and bleeds as Cobb staggers to his feet, out of breath. Cobb dusts himself down and does his hair in the mirror.

> (*at his reflection*)
> Idiot. How could you be so stupid?
> (*turns to look at the Young Man*)
> You're on your own, Billy-boy. Here . . .
> (*reaches into his pocket and pulls out a pair of rubber gloves; he tosses them at the Young Man*)
> . . . take these. Present for you, to get you started on your new solo career.

He reaches down and pulls the Young Man to his feet. The Young Man's face is a bloody mess. Cobb picks up the rubber gloves and stuffs them into the Young Man's breast pocket.

He drags the Young Man to the door.

> Now, fuck off.

He throws the Young Man out of the door and slams it behind him. He laughs hysterically as he walks back into the living room and we:

DISSOLVE TO:

INT. COBB'S LIVING ROOM – NIGHT

Cobb is lying on the floor, tossing a golfball into the air and catching it just before it hits his face.

The Blonde is sitting on the couch.

THE BLONDE

Did you have to beat him?

COBB

Did you have to sleep with him?

THE BLONDE

You told me to.

COBB

I said you should if you *had* to, that's not the same as telling
you to.

(*catches ball and looks over*)

Did you enjoy it?

THE BLONDE

Did you enjoy beating him up?

COBB

Of course.

The Blonde shakes her head pityingly.

He brought it on himself. He didn't have to tell me that he
was seeing you, but once he did I had to react the way I
would really.

He sits up.

I'm in deep shit, this has to work.

THE BLONDE

But why are you so sure they think you were involved?

COBB

They've already had me in for questioning, for Christ's sake.
They know my m.o. and it's just a matter of time before they
find the bloke who saw me leave and pull me in.

THE BLONDE

You think he got a good look at you?

COBB

No, which is why this will work; all we need is someone else with the same way of working and roughly the same appearance caught in the act.

THE BLONDE

Why can't you just tell them what really happened – that you just found her like that?

COBB

If you'd seen her, you wouldn't even ask. It was horrible, blood everywhere. Her face had been . . . beaten . . . almost not human. I'd been in the flat a while, I may have left traces, forensic stuff, I don't know. But she was fresh, she hadn't been dead long, the witness might put me there close enough to the time of death –

THE BLONDE

But if he didn't get a good look –

COBB

That's not the point! A crime that brutal, an old lady beaten like that . . . if they *think* it's me, they'll find a way to make it stick. There has to be someone else – I've told them there's someone else!

THE BLONDE

What if he has an alibi?

COBB

He's a loner, that's why he's perfect. And he looks so different now that strangers aren't going to remember having seen him. He's our man.

The Blonde and Cobb look at each other.

FADE TO BLACK.

EXT. NARROW PASSAGEWAY CONNECTING TWO STREETS LIT BY A STREETLIGHT – NIGHT

It is raining.

The Young Man (short hair, shades) stumbles along. His dark suit bulges oddly. He brings his hand up to adjust his shades and we see a fifty-pound note sticking out of his cuff.

He disappears around the corner and we:

CUT TO:

INT. LIVING ROOM – NIGHT

The Young Man has taken his suit off and is removing the money from his body. He is wet, his tie is loose, there is blood on his shirt, he is on the phone.

> YOUNG MAN
> (*strained, on edge*)

I got it.

> THE BLONDE (O.S.)

You're bringing them to me?

> YOUNG MAN
> (*bending to remove money from his leg*)

I had to stop off to dump the money.

> THE BLONDE (O.S.)

Money?

> YOUNG MAN
> (*giggling*)

Lot of fucking money!

He yelps as he yanks tape from his hairy legs.

> THE BLONDE (O.S.)

What?

> YOUNG MAN

Nothing. I'll be over soon.

> THE BLONDE (O.S.)

So it was OK?

> YOUNG MAN
> (*a pause, close to tears*)

OK, yeah. I'll be over soon.

He hangs up the phone. He's removed most of the money, but odd bundles hang from his legs and shirt.

78

He looks at the hammer lying on the floor, blood on it. Next to the hammer lies the manilla envelope.

The Young Man picks up the envelope, pauses for a moment, then rips it open and yanks out the contents: eight-by-ten glossies.

*The photos are straight modelling portrait shots of The Blonde –
absolutely nothing interesting or remarkable about them whatsoever.*

*He flips through them again and again looking for some meaning,
some super-subtle obscenity he might be missing, a manic desperate look
developing on his face.*

He flings them across the room, and we:

CUT TO:

EXT. OUTSIDE THE BLONDE'S FLAT

The Young Man looks up at the window. He's not happy.

INT. THE BLONDE'S FRONT HALL – NIGHT

The Blonde moves to answer the door.

*The door opens to reveal a wet, bedraggled Young Man, bruises on his
face. The Young Man slaps The Blonde hard and walks in past her. She
expresses neither pain nor surprise.*

> THE BLONDE
> You promised me you wouldn't look in the envelope.

> YOUNG MAN
> Wasn't sealed, they fell out.

The Blonde stares at him with a half-smile.

> THE BLONDE
> Right . . . they fell out.

The Young Man looks back at her coldly.

> YOUNG MAN
> Are you going to explain?

The Blonde says nothing.

(*rising anger*)
What?! Was it all bullshit just to get the money?

THE BLONDE
(*shrugs*)
He's never had any in there before.

The Young Man grabs her by the shoulders and shakes her.

YOUNG MAN
What, then?!!

The Blonde puts her hands up defensively to tell him to remove his hands. He does so.

THE BLONDE
(*matter-of-factly*)
For a friend. The police think he did something which he didn't and he needs a decoy – another likely suspect, someone caught robbing a place the same way he does, using his methods.

YOUNG MAN
His methods?
(*truth dawning*)
Who's the friend?

THE BLONDE
(*mischievous, waiting for a reaction*)
Cobb.

The Young Man closes his eyes.

The Blonde turns away.

(*straight*)
He broke into a flat a couple of weeks ago. Found an old lady who'd been beaten to death. He ran off, somebody saw him and a few days later the police picked him up for questioning. They think he killed her –

YOUNG MAN
(*opens eyes*)
He probably did.

THE BLONDE

He's a thief, not a murderer. He told them they had the
wrong man, had him confused with another burglar he knew
about, one who has the same m.o. . . . you.

YOUNG MAN

Why me?

THE BLONDE
(*like it's his own fault*)

You set yourself up for it. Cobb noticed you following him
days before he approached you – at first he thought you were
police but then he followed you –

YOUNG MAN

He followed *me*?

THE BLONDE
(*sarcastic*)

He followed *you* and realized that you were just some . . .
weirdo . . . waiting to be drawn into it, used.

YOUNG MAN
(*asking for it*)

So you and Cobb . . .

The Blonde shrugs and smiles.

*The Young Man slaps the wall hard by the side of The Blonde's head. She
doesn't flinch. He turns around, raising his hands in total frustration.*

How could you do this to me? To anyone?

THE BLONDE

It's not that bad. You've got that money. You didn't kill the
old woman. You're just there to plant doubt in the minds of
the police – they'll never charge you. The idea *was* that
someone would catch you breaking in tonight, the police
would pull you in, then ask you about the old lady – which
you wouldn't know anything about.

YOUNG MAN
(*incredulous*)

Yeah, but they'd still charge me with breaking and entering!

THE BLONDE
(*amused*)
But you did do that. And anyway, for whatever reason, nobody did catch you red-handed.

YOUNG MAN
(*wielding the bloody hammer*)
He came in, he went down. I didn't hang around to see if he got up. It's his blood on my hammer.
(*smashes hammer into wall*)
How could you do this to me?

THE BLONDE
(*unimpressed*)
It's not personal. When I agreed to it I didn't even know you.

The Young Man drops the hammer. The Blonde opens her eyes. The Young Man takes a deep breath, regains his composure.

YOUNG MAN
I'm going to the police in the morning.

THE BLONDE
You can't.

YOUNG MAN
I'm going and I'll tell them everything.

THE BLONDE
You can't – they'll never believe you.

YOUNG MAN
I'll tell them everything and they'll believe me because it's the truth.

THE BLONDE
They'll never believe you unless someone backs you up.

YOUNG MAN
You could.

THE BLONDE
I won't.

YOUNG MAN
(*confident*)

They'll make you. Your lies won't hold up against the truth.

The Blonde turns away, shaking her head.

THE BLONDE

You know, I really wouldn't do –

She is cut off by the sound of the door slamming. She turns to see that the Young Man has gone.

FADE TO BLACK.

INT. ROOM WITH TABLE – DAY

Close on the Young Man (short hair, bruises).

YOUNG MAN

That's it.

Wider shows us a room lit by early morning sun, the Young Man seated at a table, an Older Man opposite. Between them on the table is a tape recorder. They both look tired. The Older Man doesn't speak.

I mean . . . if you've got questions . . .

The Older Man leans forward.

OLDER MAN

One or two.

A pause. The Young Man raises his eyebrows in expectation.

CUT TO:

EXT. STREET IN THE WEST END – DAWN

Cobb strolls down the street. He is carrying the leather holdall.

CUT TO:

INT. ROOM WITH TABLE AND TAPE RECORDER – DAY

> OLDER MAN
>
> You see . . . we don't actually *have* any unsolved murders of old ladies right now.

> YOUNG MAN
> (*baffled*)
>
> But there has –

> OLDER MAN
> (*more assertive*)
>
> There is *no* such ongoing investigation.

The Young Man looks confused and scared.

> And we don't know this . . .
> (*looks at his notes*)
> . . . 'Cobb' of yours.

CUT TO:

INT. THE BLONDE'S FRONT HALL – DAY

The Blonde opens the front door to Cobb, and we:

DISSOLVE TO:

INT. THE BLONDE'S LIVING ROOM – DAY

The Blonde and Cobb are having a drink.

> COBB
>
> I warned you he'd look in the envelope.

> THE BLONDE
>
> He gave me his word. I believed him.

> COBB
>
> Nothing personal, he couldn't help himself – he's a born peeper. Anyway, down to business.

> THE BLONDE
>
> Business?

Cobb takes a handkerchief out of his pocket and starts to wipe the outside of his glass, and we:

CUT TO:

INT. ROOM WITH TABLE — DAY

We move in on the Young Man, puzzled, thinking hard.

OLDER MAN (O.S.)

Perhaps there's something else you'd like to tell me about.

CUT TO:

INT. THE BLONDE'S LIVING ROOM — DAY

The Blonde watches, puzzled, as Cobb stretches his rubber gloves and puts them on, interlacing his fingers for a snug fit.

COBB

Where's the hammer?

THE BLONDE

Oh, down there in the bag.

She points to a shopping bag on the table across the room from Cobb. Cobb rises, crosses the room and picks up the bag with his back to The Blonde. She can't see him take it out of the bag and look at the dried blood on its head.

What are you going to do with it?

COBB
(his back to her)

The old man was pretty specific about the way I should do things.

THE BLONDE
(puzzled)

What's he have to say about it?

COBB
(turning around, hammer in hand)

Well, he *is* giving me all of that money out of his safe.

THE BLONDE
(*not liking this*)

Money? What for?

CUT TO:

INT. ROOM WITH TABLE — DAY

Close on the Young Man as he thinks.

The Older Man puts on a pair of rubber surgical gloves.

OLDER MAN (O.S.)

Anything at all. *Your* side of things.

CUT TO:

INT. THE BLONDE'S LIVING ROOM — DAY

Cobb moves towards The Blonde with the hammer.

COBB
(*smiling*)

He says your demands have become unreasonable . . . too
greedy in your blackmail.

THE BLONDE
(*scared now*)

But, no – I, I, I don't –

COBB
(*smiling, soothing*)

Something about an incident you witnessed in this very
room? He was specific about where and how I should take
care of things. Some sense of poetic justice, I suppose.

THE BLONDE

But I –

COBB

Something about a bloodstained carpet you've got stashed
away to back up your story, should it ever be told.

The Blonde is crying.

THE BLONDE

How could you do this to me?

COBB
(*softly*)

Money.

He lunges for The Blonde, grabbing her wrist and pulling her to the floor. He forces her hand flat against the floor and raises the hammer high above his head, and we:

CUT TO:

INT. ROOM WITH TABLE — DAY

Close on the Young Man as he realizes something.

YOUNG MAN

Did you talk to her?

OLDER MAN
(*nods gravely*)

We found her early this morning.

YOUNG MAN

Found her?

OLDER MAN

Her body.

The Young Man covers his face with his hands.

We also found a hammer with two types of blood on it, one type which I assume will match the bloke you put in hospital. All of her fingers were smashed – you must have tortured her for the combination.

YOUNG MAN

NO! I haven't done anything to her! Go and pick up Cobb, he did it, he must have done it –

The Older Man silences the Young Man by putting a shoebox on to the table between them.

OLDER MAN
(*rifling through the contents of the box*)
We found some interesting items at your flat. In addition to
the various items which the deceased reported stolen last
week, we found several pairs of ladies' underwear – are they
hers?

The Young Man says nothing.

I assume so, since they were found stashed with some
passport-style photographs of the deceased.

The Young Man closes his eyes.

(*pulls a small, clear plastic bag from the box*)
We also found this pearl earring.

*The Young Man opens his eyes. He looks at the evidence bag which the
Older Man is holding out for him to see. Inside it is The Blonde's pearl
earring.*

It matches the one worn by the deceased at the time of her
death. Little trophy?

YOUNG MAN
(*desperation*)
NO! Cobb planted it! He took it when we broke in – pick
him up, I gave you his address, he's the one who killed her –
he has to be!

OLDER MAN
We went to the address you gave us. There's no 'Cobb' there.
The flat belongs to a . . .
(*checks notes*)
. . . Timothy Kerr. He just got back from holiday and he says
that he was robbed while he was away. Not too much was
taken . . . but his new credit card hasn't arrived –

YOUNG MAN
That was Cobb, see?! We used it to buy a meal one time!

*The Older Man reaches into the box and pulls out another clear evi-
dence bag. Inside it is a credit card.*

OLDER MAN

We found this at your flat.

YOUNG MAN
(running out of steam)

It was . . . Cobb who stole it . . .

The Older Man flips the card over to display the signature on the back.

OLDER MAN

Is this your handwriting?

The Young Man looks at the card in despair.

YOUNG MAN
(quiet)

Yes.

CUT TO:

EXT. BUSY WEST END STREET CROWDED WITH PEDESTRIANS — DAY

Cobb comes out of a café and walks away from us down the street.

He stops and looks back towards us over his shoulder as if to check that no one is following him.

Satisfied, he turns back, moves off and is swallowed by the mass of pedestrians crossing the frame in slo-mo and we:

FADE TO BLACK.

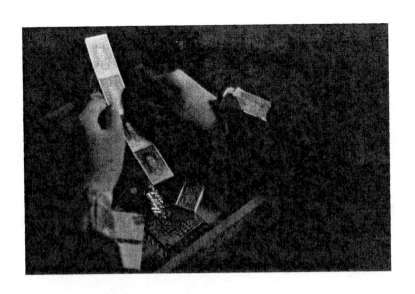

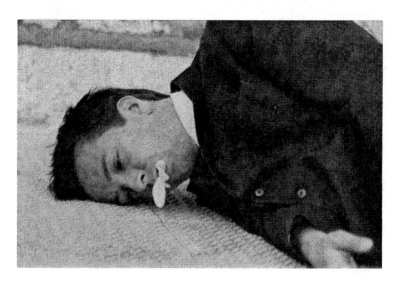

FOLLOWING ON:
Christopher Nolan and Jeremy Theobald
interviewed by James Mottram

'The following is my explanation . . . well, more of an account of
what happened.'

Like the film itself, the first words spoken in Christopher Nolan's
Following are pregnant with double meaning. His head spinning
with notions of truth, would-be writer Bill (as he calls himself),
now at a point of confession, must clarify his disclosures. How
did he get himself into this mess, this world of duplicity? The 'following', of course, the act of tailing individuals for the purposes
of research. After all, who hasn't listened to someone's conversation on the bus or spied on someone from a tall building? It's
what led him to the enigmatic burglar Cobb, right? And the set-
up? But words, whether spoken or heard, are, like the objects
placed by Cobb in the box in the opening credits, lethal self-
entrapment for the inexperienced and the naive.

By comparison, Bill's gestures, suggestively sewn through the
fabric of the film, are as empty as the derelict buildings Cobb
inhabits. From his tip-tapping of the typewriter keys, proudly
proclaiming he's a writer, to his similarly notional efforts with a
tuning fork at the piano, we know he's no artist, merely someone
with a romantic vision brought on by living in a garret for too
long. His efforts to deflect suspicion after he has gained a taste for
breaking and entering – a new suit, a shave and a haircut – are,
too, ultimately meaningless; reinforcing his physical proximity to
Cobb, they photo-fit him even more perfectly for the role of burglar than if he'd had a bag with 'swag' written on it. Innocent,
perhaps, like the signing of the credit card, but incriminating
nonetheless. His pursuit of The Blonde, the victim of his and
Cobb's third illegal collaboration, while heartfelt, is equally
insignificant in the scheme of things; love, after all, is a notion for-
eign to this amoral world. Even his escape route after he and
Cobb abort their first robbery together is a dead-end, while the
Batman sign on his door conferring super-heroic status . . . well,
that's just laughable. Remember, this is a man who sellotapes

wads of cash to his arms as a means of carrying them, looking like Frankenstein's monster as he waddles away. His only important gesture is one of transgression. Breaking the social taboo of spying on people is Bill's first, and most important, violation, leading him inexorably to the role of housebreaker.

It is Cobb, the charismatic gremlin of the piece, whose actions are more effective. He's the break-in artist who perches on Bill's shoulder, urging him to follow suit and do wrong. Whether he's setting you up for infidelity, misplacing your earring or shaking up your can of beer, his mischief has a pervasive, yet beguiling, effect. From his out-of-tune ditty on the same piano keyboard Bill uses, to the candid revelations of his methodology later used to frame his pupil, Cobb is teasing us, and his opposite number, with the knowledge that he's the bad guy of the piece. He might call The Blonde 'a fox', but it is he who out-foxes everyone naive enough to trust his words. Unbeknownst to Bill, he trains the would-be writer in his *modus operandi* to set him up as a decoy suspect in a brutal murder case which the burglar claims to have stumbled upon. The signs were there, of course; the rotting corpse of a dead bird in Cobb's lock-up seems to foreshadow the impending doom. By the time we reach the final, haunting, shot of Cobb evaporating in a crowded Covent Garden street, not unlike Keyser Soze's vanishing act in the denouement to *The Usual Suspects*, Bill has found himself inextricably indicted for something much more deadly. He has become the victim of the burglar, the man who plays God, who recites the mantra 'You take it away, you show them what they had' as he does. By the end, it's a phrase that fits Bill, no longer in possession of his freedom, as tightly as Cobb's white gloves slip over his hands.

While Christopher Nolan's seventy-four-minute black-and-white micro-budget directorial début borrows from both the players and the confessional nature of the traditional *film noir*, what makes it so refreshing is its economic appropriation of the genre. Words may be deadly in the plot, but Nolan treats them with similar respect. Not a syllable is wasted (nor indeed a frame of film, with Nolan rejecting establishing shots), a fact that is undoubtedly partially testament to the restrictive conditions under which the film was made. Yet *Following*, suitably enough, is a very deceptive affair. Ivan Cornell's shadowy lighting, David

Julyan's evocative score, Tristan Martin's spare-but-spot-on art direction and Nolan's own cinematography masterfully combine to create production values Hollywood studios would spend thousands to create.

Technically adept, the film is bolstered by Nolan's own sense of how to create an atmosphere on a shoestring. Filming London as refreshingly as Mike Leigh did in *Naked*, roof-tops and sky fill the frames, not shots of Eros and Buck House. It's an unfamiliarity that matches the sharp-witted but antiquated dialogue. While characters will finish each other's sentences, their colloquialisms – Cobb uses the near-defunct word 'saucy' on more than one occasion – lend the film definition.

As does the form. Told via a unique cut-up structure that runs three time-lines concurrently, *Following* eschews the controlled narrative chaos of, say, Nic Roeg's *Performance* or *Bad Timing*, in favour of a highly organized, if initially disorientating, means of story-telling. Enticing the audience to play detective, the film forces you to piece the jigsaw together, releasing information in much the same fractured way as we would encounter it in our day-to-day lives. Our first port of call is the model mannequin on Bill's shelf; broken by Cobb, we have already encountered a scene chronologically later to that where The Blonde picks it up, only for it to fall apart because of its damaged condition. Put this together with the three guises Bill sports throughout – greasy, clean-shaven and bruised – and the scenes dutifully reorder themselves in our minds.

It all makes *Following* an almost unique experience in cinema. While fans of *Clerks* and *El Mariachi* (both costlier than Nolan's film) carefully guard the no-budget accolade for their beloved films, *Following* is a wholly more satisfying and complex ride, emotionally and aesthetically. Its achievement, betraying the notion that film-making is for those with a degree from film school, is on the screen for all to see. The following, an interview between myself, writer-director Christopher Nolan and actor-producer Jeremy Theobald, who plays Bill, is their explanation. Well, more of an account of what happened . . .

JAMES MOTTRAM: *What was the starting point for* Following*?*
CHRISTOPHER NOLAN: It was a combination of things, the primary

one being living in a crowded part of the West End, near Tottenham Court Road, where you would be constantly surrounded by people. I would pick out individuals and wonder how they had arrived at this particular spot and where were they going. Once you start doing that, once you start considering the other people around you as individuals, you start to think about the voluntary protocols that a city like London has developed to preserve the individuality of people in close proximity to strangers. One example is that you don't walk at the same pace as a stranger if you're walking down Oxford Street or somewhere. It's very natural to vary your pace from a stranger, because otherwise it seems suspicious. I found myself looking at that notion a lot. I'd been burgled a couple of years before, when I lived in Camden, and seeing a door broken down, you realize that the door wasn't ever keeping anybody out. When someone just decides to invade your space, it's really very shocking. I decided to put the two together. The one is the natural extreme, the logical extension of the other.

JM: *How did you get involved?*
JEREMY THEOBALD: Chris and I were both at college at the University of London, but we didn't start working together until after we both graduated. He ran the film society, and I ran the drama society. He saw me act on stage several times. I'd always wanted to get into doing some film acting. Finally, I was presented with a short film script called *Larceny*, which Christopher had written. It was the first short film script that I read that had a plot to it – a beginning, middle and end, and a really nice twist. We made that together and used it as a test bed for working with a small crew. Again, black and white, hand-held camera, 16mm. We wanted to see whether we could shoot on a weekend, then edit it. It came out well and went to the Cambridge Film Festival. We then did a three-minute short, *Doodlebug*, and then we collaborated on *Following*. He presented me with the lead part, which was written for me on the basis of working with him on the other two films. He asked me to co-produce the film with him and his then-girlfriend-now-wife Emma, because I knew a lot of actors.

JM: *Where did you meet the rest of the cast and crew?*
JT: We were all at UCL. I was studying Physiology; Chris was doing English; Emma was doing History; Lucy, who plays The

Blonde, was doing Italian; Alex, who plays Cobb, was doing Architecture. None of us had any formal training in film. We just collaborated together as a learning process, to see if we could make a feature film and whether it would be any good.

JM: *It's a story about violation, isn't it?*
CN: Yes. For the Young Man at the centre of the story, who – in the process of violation – crosses this line by imposing himself on others by following them, it's such a seemingly harmless thing to engage in. Once he's broken that rule, he breaks more and more.

JM: *Do you think your character is naive?*
JT: I don't think he's naive. He gets set up in a way that would be more or less impossible for anybody to work out in that situation. He's meeting brand-new people in a brand-new environment. He is a loner and has been by himself for a long time. He does fall in love with a beautiful woman, and he's in an environment which is completely unfamiliar to him. Anybody can get lost in that environment.

JM: *You paint a fascinating, and unusual, picture of London . . .*
CN: I became very struck by the empty spaces above shops. London is the city where no one looks up. It's all on ground level. You actually wind up finding some interesting spaces above, below and behind street level. The various roof-top scenes were a way of distinguishing more unusual, more private spaces.
JT: An awful lot of films shot in London go down the unfortunate road of making sure they can sell in the US, doing picture-postcard shots of driving past Tower Bridge or going around Trafalgar Square. What the film does show of London is a lot of backstreets, a lot of sky – London's typical grey skies. It's been compared to Antonioni's *Blow Up* in that sense.

JM: *How do you explain the complex narrative structure?*
CN: The film, for me, takes a logical approach to developing a story. My most useful definition of narrative is that it's a controlled release of information. You don't feel any obligation to release that information on a chronological basis. What's interesting about doing this is trying to expand the story in all directions. To me, that's the way we receive stories in everyday life. A newspaper gives you a headline, and the process of reading the article

is a process of expanding the story. The follow-up story next day would then increase your understanding further, and I wanted to take that approach to the structure of the film. I guess you could call it anecdotal.

JT: The best analogy you worked out was *The Jerry Springer Show*, which sounds rather improbable, but it does work incredibly well. You get one guest telling their side of the story; another guest comes on and completely challenges that story, filling in the background. The third guest comes on and does exactly the same. That sort of dynamic is what drives the film forward and what ultimately makes people interested in finding out what happens at the end.

JM: *How do you explain the ending?*

CN: *Following* has a very tight conclusion. I have to confess – as was pointed out in a very good review I read of the film on-line – that the tidy ending runs somewhat counter to the kind of puzzling ambiguity that's there the whole way through the film. There's a sense in which that's true; there's a flourish at the end of the film that tidies things up.

JM: *You seem to crave the freedom a novelist has.*

CN: Yes. Structure would never be questioned there. It's just accepted. If a novel wants to tell a story in a non-chronological way, that's just one of the things you're allowed to do. I think film has had that potential since way back. Think of *Citizen Kane* now. The narrative structure is incredibly inventive. Every other aspect of film-making, since that film, has advanced enormously. I now have incredible editing freedom that people making films back then didn't have. I can have an incredibly fractured *mise-en-scène* that people can put together like that. But narratively, things are simpler now than they were back then. I really think it's TV that's at fault.

JM: *Why?*

CN: TV has held back narrative developments. It's entirely linear. It has to be. It's changing now, but you have to be able to watch the last ten minutes where they explain the whole story so that you are narratively satisfied. Once VHS came along, you could control the time-line – while you watched it.

JM: *Were you influenced by any other works in particular?*
CN: Graham Swift's novel *Waterland*. I read it when I was at school. I was very struck by the way he created these parallel time-lines and jumped between them. He has an incredible structural approach to these time-lines, clueing you into what's going on so much that by the end of the book he's leaving sentences half-finished and you know where they're going. With films, I was very taken with the work of Alan Parker – particularly *The Wall* – and John Frankenheimer's *Seconds*.

JM: *You shot the film at weekends, for a period of over a year. How was that?*
CN: It was a process of stamina, getting out of bed at 8 o'clock on a Saturday morning. It was all about creating energy. It was a very grinding process as we were all working through the week doing really hard jobs. And though it's very exciting on the first couple of shoots you do, you then get into that tedium of just getting through. During the shoot, I did my utmost to strip away worthless material, any padding. It's a very bare-bones style.

JM: *How difficult was it to maintain your performance over such a protracted period of time?*
JT: It was actually fairly easy. We shot most Saturdays, and every Friday night I would go out, get drunk, get up early on Saturday, have my McDonalds' breakfast, and as soon as I put that suit on and got to the location with a bunch of people that I didn't see during the week, then I just started behaving like the character.

JM: *Do you recall any problems during the shoot?*
JT: We did have one problem, which we call 'the definition of irony'. When my character and Cobb burgle the girl's flat, we steal a load of stuff, and I'm seen putting them in a bag . . . well, all these props were actual items from Chris's parents' house in Highgate. They were to be used in a scene later when I take them out of the bag and look at photos of her. There was a gap in between shooting the burglary scene and this scene; in between, Chris's parents were burgled, and some of the items I put in the bag were stolen. We couldn't bring out all of the items in the bag, because some of them had been stolen. That's our definition of irony.

JM: *How was the film funded?*
CN: I paid for it myself. I was working as a media trainer at the time, and I would buy a roll of film a week and then process it.

JM: *Had you tried to get money from other sources?*
JT: We'd explored getting money from people in the past. In this country, if you haven't got any training and you're not introduced by somebody, then people are extremely cautious about seeing you – let alone reading your script or giving you money. We wanted to become film-makers, and so we thought it would be easier if we made films, rather than spending two years trying to raise money for a film that might never get made.

JM: *Despite the low budget, the film still retains high production values. How so?*
JT: Through a sense of continuity gained through working with an extremely small group of people. Usually, most scenes were me, another actor, Chris as director, a lighting guy and a gaffer. We used to be able to get all of us, and all of the equipment, in a London taxi to go to the location. Also, being able to see the rushes, once they've been processed, to make sure that everything was in the right place if we were going back to a location that Saturday. In a strange way, the sense of time made everything a lot less rushed, which meant there were probably fewer mistakes made than there would've been if we'd shot every day on a three-week schedule. We were incredibly careful with how much film we used and how many takes we did. Most shots we did in only two takes. We got it right first time, and then we did a second one for insurance and coverage. We knew our lines back to front, and to a certain extent we could improvise if it became necessary.

JM: *How did you set about getting costumes, locations, etc.?*
JT: Sets were people's houses and flats. My flat is used, Chris's parents' house is used. Costumes were our own clothes. The suit that I wear is my Dad's wedding suit from the 1960s.

JM: *How fast was the editing process?*
CN: We had to shoot in such a specific way that my rough cut was pulled together in a few days. I was able to take a week, get a tape on the Tuesday and edit it together in my mind during the week. I enjoyed the later stages, when I brought the editor Gareth Heal

on board. That's when we started to experiment, to really try and maximize the effects of the structure.

JM: *Does the finished version differ greatly from the screenplay?*
CN: The original screenplay is pretty close to the finished film. The basic structure was always there. The script is more complex. We showed it to some people, and got comments, and decided at the very last minute that instead of rapidly trying to, as it were, teach the audience the structure at the beginning, what instead was probably best was to take a little longer to introduce the characters. Later in the film, we similarly experimented and changed the order of certain blocks of narrative. The third time-line, where the Young Man is bruised and planning the robbery, we wound up not shooting as extensively. It gave us a certain amount of freedom to reorder scenes towards the end of the film. The scene, for example, where The Blonde is enticing the Young Man to commit the robbery for her: I felt in the script you didn't yet know that the robbery was going to go wrong. It definitely played best when you knew she was up to something and you saw her in a way the Young Man doesn't. That was the kind of reordering that we played with.

JM: *Were the difficulties inherent in the distribution process a shock?*
CN: It certainly wasn't a shock. We went into this film really as amateurs, really as people who just wanted to make a film. I was very careful never to raise any false hopes or expectations with people. When it came to the question of distribution, to us it was pretty miraculous. It was one step even further than we'd expected to go. I was never expecting to be able to take the film as far as we did.

JM: *How did you manage to ready the film for distribution?*
JT: We were incredibly lucky to be picked up by Next Wave Films in the US, who provide finishing funds for films. Their president is Peter Broderick, who saw it shortly after the San Francisco Film Festival. He picked up the film then, and with his company the film got a new sound mix and a 35mm blow-up. He took us to the Toronto Film Festival, where we managed to sell the distribution rights for the US, France and the UK. Without his help, it would have been extremely difficult.

JM: *How do you think the industry took to* Following?

JT: To the film industry, this film came completely out of the blue. Nobody had seen it in development or production for two years. We had just been touting it round festivals and trying to sell it to distributors during that time. Everyone was a bit surprised by it.

JM: *The film only received a limited UK release. Were you still sent scripts despite few people seeing the movie?*

CN: I was, because more people saw it in America. But I certainly didn't get any scripts from English companies. I'm always asked, 'Why are you working in America now?' It's only very recently that I've had any interest from English companies. The release was not great, but, to be honest, it's an on-going struggle that film-makers have. There are very few happy independent film-makers.

Memento

CAST AND CREW

MAIN CAST

LEONARD SHELBY	Guy Pearce
NATALIE	Carrie-Anne Moss
TEDDY	Joe Pantoliano
BURT	Mark Boone Junior
SAMMY	Stephen Tobolowsky
MRS JANKIS	Harriet Sansom Harris
DODD	Callum Keith Rennie
WAITER	Russ Fega
BLONDE	Kimberly Campbell
JIMMY GRANTZ	Larry Holden
CATHERINE SHELBY	Jorja Fox
DOCTOR	Thomas Lennon
TATTOOIST	Marianne Muellerleile

MAIN CREW

Directed by	Christopher Nolan
Screenplay by	Christopher Nolan
Based on a Short Story by	Jonathan Nolan
Produced by	Suzanne Todd
	Jennifer Todd
Executive Producer	Aaron Ryder
Co-executive Producers	William Tyrer
	Chris J. Ball
Co-producer	Elaine Dysinger
Associate Producer	Emma Thomas
Original Music by	David Julyan
Cinematography by	Wally Pfister
Film Editing by	Dody Dorn
Casting by	John Papsidera
Production Design by	Patti Podesta
Costume Design by	Cindy Evans

FADE IN:

INT. DERELICT HOUSE – DAY [COLOUR SEQUENCE]

A Polaroid photograph, clasped between finger and thumb, showing a crude, crime-scene flash picture of a man's body lying on a decaying wooden floor, a bloody mess where his head should be.

The image in the photo starts to fade as we superimpose titles. The hand holding the photo suddenly fans it in a rapid flapping motion, then holds it still. The image fades more, and again the picture is fanned.

As titles end the image fades to nothing. The hand holding the photo flaps it again, then places it at the front of a Polaroid camera.

The camera sucks the blank picture up, then the flash goes off.

The Polaroid camera is lowered, revealing the sweaty, heavy-breathing face of Leonard (mid-30s). There are droplets of blood across his face. Leonard stares, satisfied, at something on the ground in front of him. There is wet blood on his blue shirt and beige suit. His hand opens and catches a handgun that leaps up into his grasp.

Still staring, he crouches down and pulls a body off the floor by the wet hair of its bloody head. He slowly inserts the barrel of the gun into the bloody mess where the mouth should be.

Leonard flinches. A deafening roar as wet red leaps off his face and suit and the head, with a spasm, reassembles itself into the face of Teddy (40s, moustache) and we:

CUT TO:

INT. MOTEL ROOM 21 – DAY [BLACK-AND-WHITE SEQUENCE]

Close on Leonard's eyes. He rolls them to one side, then turns his head.

LEONARD (V.O.)

So where are you?

He lifts his head. He is lying on a queen-sized bed.

You're in some motel room.

CUT TO:

EXT. DERELICT BUILDING — DAY [COLOUR SEQUENCE]

A late-model Jaguar bumps across some railroad tracks and approaches a large, clearly abandoned derelict building. Leonard is driving. He wears a beige suit and blue shirt (no blood). Next to him is Teddy. Leonard stops the car next to a pick-up truck sitting outside the derelict building. He kills the engine, staring at the pick-up.

LEONARD

Looks like somebody's home.

Teddy looks from Leonard to the pick-up and back.

TEDDY

That thing's been here for years.

Leonard gets out of the Jaguar and moves to the pick-up. He inspects it with a methodical, practiced eye. Teddy follows.

LEONARD

I think you're wrong. These tracks aren't more than a few days old.

He opens the door of the pick-up and searches the interior. On the dirty vinyl of the passenger seat he finds six bullets. Leonard picks two of them up and studies them. He drops them on to the dashboard, then shuts the door.

Let's take a look inside.

He walks towards the house, patting his jacket pockets. Teddy leans on the pick-up, uneasy, watching Leonard.

INT. DERELICT BUILDING — DAY

Leonard stands in the dimly lit, decaying former hallway. He pulls a stack of Polaroid photographs out of his pocket and leafs through them as Teddy starts walking towards him.

Leonard finds a photo showing Teddy with a shit-eating grin standing in front of the pick-up truck. On the broad white strip beneath the photo is handwritten:
'TEDDY GAMMELL TEL. 555 0134'.

He flips the photo over. On the white strip on the back, in the same small handwriting:
'DON'T BELIEVE HIS LIES'
'HE IS THE ONE'
'KILL HIM'.

LEONARD (V.O.)

I've finally found him. How long have I been looking?

He stuffs the Polaroids back into his pocket, reaches around to the back of his waistband and draws a handgun, keeping it out of Teddy's line of sight. Teddy enters, wary.

TEDDY

Find anything? Didn't think so. Let's go, yeah?

Leonard neither replies nor turns around. Teddy, worried, affects a casual air, shrugging dismissively.

Fuck this.

He turns and heads for the door. Leonard leaps on him, pistol-whipping him furiously as he shouts:

LEONARD

YOU PAY FOR WHAT YOU DID! YOU BEG FOR-
GIVENESS, THEN YOU PAY!

Teddy is down. Leonard drags him back, deeper into the dark house. He is in a frenzy. He dumps Teddy at the end of the hall and stands over him. Teddy spits blood.

TEDDY

You don't have a clue, you freak.

Leonard crouches down and grabs Teddy by the lapels.

LEONARD

Beg my forgiveness! Beg my wife's forgiveness before I blow your brains out!

TEDDY

Leonard, you don't have a clue what's going on. You don't even know my name.

LEONARD
(*triumphant smile*)

Teddy!

TEDDY

You read it off your fucking photo. You don't know me, you don't even know who you are.

LEONARD

I'm Leonard Shelby, I'm from San Francisco and I'm –

TEDDY
(*bloody grin*)

That's who you *were*, you don't know who you *are*.

LEONARD

Shut your mouth!

TEDDY

Lemme take you down in the basement and show you what you've become.

He gestures towards the basement door, in pain, but enjoying Leonard's growing anxiety.

(*intimate*)

C'mon, Lenny – we'll take a look down there together. Then you'll know. You'll know what you really are.

Leonard glances fearfully at the door, then looks at Teddy. He thrusts the barrel of his gun into Teddy's mouth and we are at the shot from the end of the opening sequence. Teddy panics, shaking his head, trying to talk around the metal, but gags just as Leonard pulls the trigger. A shot rings out as we:

CUT TO:

INT. MOTEL ROOM 21 – DAY [BLACK-AND-WHITE SEQUENCE]

Leonard lies on the queen-sized bed. He lifts his head.

> LEONARD (V.O.)
> So you're in some motel room . . .

He gets up, surveys the room as if for the first time. He wears boxers and a plaid work shirt.

> . . . you don't know how long you've been there or how you
> got there . . .

There is a room key on the dresser. The plastic tag identifies it as the key to room 21. Leonard opens drawers in the room.

> Just some anonymous motel room. Won't tell you anything.
> Nothing in the drawers, but you look anyway.

He reaches for the bedside-table drawer.

> Nothing except the Gideon Bible.

He opens the drawer to find a Gideon Bible.

> CUT TO:

INT. DISCOUNT INN OFFICE – DAY [COLOUR SEQUENCE]

Extreme close-up of fingers rifling bills in a wallet. Leonard counts out some money and hands it to the fat, sweaty, middle-aged man behind the counter (Burt). Burt takes the money, spotting something over Leonard's shoulder.

> BURT
> That guy's here already.

Burt taps the Polaroid photograph of Teddy, which is sitting on the counter. Leonard picks up the photo and turns to see Teddy approaching the glass door of the office. Leonard watches carefully as Teddy shambles up to the office door. A bell chimes as Teddy enters and breaks into his shit-eating grin. Leonard slips the photo into his pocket.

> TEDDY
> Lenny!

Leonard nods in apparent recognition, wary.

> LEONARD
> It's Leonard . . . like I told you before.

Teddy pretends to think hard.

> TEDDY
> Did you? I musta forgot. I'm Teddy.

> LEONARD
> *(smiles)*
> I guess I've told you about my condition.

Teddy grins and holds the door open for Leonard.

> TEDDY
> Only every time I see ya!

EXT. DISCOUNT INN CAR PARK — DAY

Teddy starts for a grey sedan. Leonard pauses behind him.

> LEONARD
> *My* car.

Teddy glances back in surprise.

> TEDDY
> This is your car.

> LEONARD
> *(shakes head)*
> You're in a playful mood.

He holds up a Polaroid of a late-model Jaguar.

> Shouldn't make fun of somebody's handicap.

Teddy smiles and heads for the brand-new Jaguar parked several cars further down.

> TEDDY
> Just trying to have a little fun.

INT. CAR – DAY

Leonard drives, Teddy admires the new car's interior, reaching down around the seats, exploring the car with his hands.

TEDDY

Roll your window up, will ya?

Leonard hits his window button. A few fragments of safety glass rise out of the door, remnants of a broken window.

LEONARD

It's broken.

Teddy looks, curious.

TEDDY

I can get that fixed for you.

Leonard shrugs.

So where are we going, Sherlock?

Leonard fishes a note out of his pocket.

LEONARD

I got a lead on a place.

He checks the note, then hands it to Teddy.

TEDDY
(*surprised at the note*)
What the hell you want to go there for?

LEONARD

You know it?

TEDDY

Yeah, it's just this fucked-up building. Why are we going there?

LEONARD
(*smiling*)

I don't remember.

EXT. DERELICT BUILDING — DAY — CONTINUOUS

The Jaguar crosses the railroad tracks and approaches the derelict building. Leonard stops the car next to the pick-up truck and kills the engine, staring at the pick-up.

LEONARD
Looks like somebody's home.

INT. MOTEL ROOM 21 — DAY [BLACK-AND-WHITE SEQUENCE]

Leonard, wearing boxers and plaid work shirt, takes the Gideon Bible out of the open bedside-table drawer.

LEONARD (V.O.)
Nothing except the Gideon Bible.

He leafs through a couple of pages, then drops the Bible back into the drawer and shuts it. He notices a message written on the back of his hand:
'REMEMBER SAMMY JANKIS'.

Sammy Jankis had the same problem. He tried writing himself notes. Lots of notes. But he'd get confused.

He licks his thumb, and rubs at the writing. To his surprise, it does not even smudge.

He notices his bare legs. There is a note taped to his right thigh with a handwritten message:
'SHAVE'.

Leonard pulls the note off, studying it carefully.

CUT TO:

INT. DISCOUNT INN ROOM 304 — DAY [COLOUR SEQUENCE]

Close on the Polaroid of Teddy. Leonard flips it over. On the back are the messages:
'DON'T BELIEVE HIS LIES'
'HE IS THE ONE'.

Leonard writes another message beneath these two:
'KILL HIM'.

He sticks the photo of Teddy between his teeth as he holds his handgun up and checks that it is loaded. He sticks the gun in the back of his waistband, the photo in his jacket pocket, and slings the Polaroid camera over his shoulder.

EXT. DISCOUNT INN – DAY

Leonard leaves room 304 and heads to the office. He pauses just outside the glass door, breathing, psyching himself up.

INT. DISCOUNT INN OFFICE – DAY

Leonard enters, confident, smiling at the man behind the desk, Burt. Burt smiles back.

> BURT

Hiya.

> LEONARD

I'm Mr Shelby from 304.

> BURT

What can I do for you, Leonard?

> LEONARD

I'm sorry . . . um . . .?

> BURT

Burt.

> LEONARD

Burt, I'm not sure, but I may have asked you to hold my calls –

> BURT

You don't know?

> LEONARD

I think I may have. I'm not good on the phone.

> BURT
> *(nods)*

You said you like to look people in the eye when you talk to them. Don't you remember?

LEONARD

That's the thing. I have this condition.

BURT

Condition?

LEONARD

I have no memory.

BURT

Amnesia?

LEONARD

No. It's different. I have no *short-term* memory. I know who I am and all about myself, but since my injury I can't make any new memories. Everything fades. If we talk for too long, I'll forget how we started. I don't know if we've ever met before and the next time I see you I won't remember this conversation. So if I seem strange or rude, that's probably . . .

He notices that Burt is staring at him as if he were an exotic insect.

I've told you this before, haven't I?

BURT
(*nods*)

I don't mean to mess with you. It's just so weird. You don't remember me at all, and we talked a bunch of times.

Leonard shrugs.

What's the last thing you remember?

Leonard looks through Burt, thinking.

LEONARD

My wife.

BURT
(*fascinated*)

What's it like?

LEONARD

Like waking. Like you always just woke up.

BURT

That must suck. All . . . backwards.

Leonard raises his eyebrows in enquiry.

Well, like . . . you gotta pretty good idea of what you're
gonna do next, but no idea what you just did.
(*chuckles*)
I'm the exact opposite.

LEONARD
(*focuses on Burt*)
How long have I been here?

BURT

Couple of days.

LEONARD
So you're holding my calls?

BURT

As requested.

Leonard reaches into his pocket and pulls out his Polaroids.

LEONARD
OK, but this guy's an exception.

*He places the Polaroid of Teddy on the counter in front of Burt. Burt
looks at it.*

Know this guy?

BURT

Your friend, right?

LEONARD
What makes you think he's my friend?

BURT

Seen you together, that's all.

LEONARD
He's not my friend, Burt. But if he calls, or if he turns up
here, then you give me a call in my room, OK?

> BURT

Sure. But nobody else, right?

> LEONARD

Just this guy.

He indicates the Polaroid of Teddy.

I hope my condition won't be a problem for you.

> BURT

Not if you remember to pay your bill.

Leonard smiles and reaches into his wallet.

Extreme close-up of fingers rifling bills in a wallet. Leonard counts out some money and hands it to Burt. Burt takes the money, spotting something over Leonard's shoulder.

That guy's here already.

He taps the Polaroid photograph of Teddy, which is sitting on the counter. Leonard picks up the photo and turns to see Teddy approaching the glass door of the office.

CUT TO:

INT. MOTEL ROOM 21 – DAY [BLACK-AND-WHITE SEQUENCE]

Leonard, in boxer shorts and plaid work shirt, rips the note from his thigh. The note says 'SHAVE'.

INT. MOTEL ROOM 21 BATHROOM – DAY

Leonard enters, and sees a white paper bag on the counter by the sink. On the bag is a handwritten message:
'SHAVE THIGH'.

He looks into the bag, then pulls out a can of shaving foam and a pack of disposable razors. He runs the hot water, steps back and lifts his foot on to the sink. He is awkward and uncomfortable. He notices an ice bucket by the sink.

INT. MOTEL ROOM 21 – DAY

Leonard sits on the bed applying shaving foam to his thigh. The ice bucket sits on the bedside table, steaming. He starts awkwardly shaving his right thigh. The phone rings and he flinches, nicking his leg. He looks at the phone, then reaches for the receiver.

INT. RESTAURANT RESTROOM – DAY [COLOUR SEQUENCE]

Leonard, in beige suit and blue shirt, flushes the urinal, then moves to the sink and starts washing his hands. He notices a message written on the back of his hand:
'REMEMBER SAMMY JANKIS'.

He stares at the message for a second, thoughtful, then tries to scrub the writing off his skin. To his surprise, it is indelible. He looks at it, quizzical, then notices some markings on his wrist, pulling his sleeve back to get a better look. He can read the start of a message:
'THE FACTS:'.

He is about to roll his sleeve up further when the restroom door opens and a man enters. Leonard dries his hands, then exits the restroom.

INT. RESTAURANT – DAY

Leonard emerges into the waiting area of a crowded restaurant. He glances around, lost, then pulls out his Polaroids, flipping through them. Someone taps him on his shoulder, and he turns to see the smiling face of a Waiter.

WAITER
Sir? You left these at your table.

Leonard looks down. The Waiter hands him a brown envelope and a motel-room key (Discount Inn, room 304). On the envelope is a handwritten message:
'FOR LEONARD, FROM NATALIE'.

Leonard looks at his Polaroid of the outside of the Discount Inn motel. There is an address written beneath it (7254 Lincoln Street).

LEONARD
Thanks. Lincoln Street?

The Waiter glances at his Polaroid.

                    WAITER
You wanna go east on sixth.
                  (*points*)
Just keep straight, all the way out of town, then take a right.

EXT./INT. JAGUAR — DAY

Leonard drives, consulting his Polaroids.

EXT. DISCOUNT INN ROOM 304 — DAY

Leonard, brown envelope in hand, finds the door to room 304.

INT. DISCOUNT INN ROOM 304 — DAY

*Leonard enters, looks around as if for the first time. An anonymous
motel room, except that tacked to one wall is a hand-drawn chart
showing the layout of some streets, and stuck to the edges of the chart
are Polaroid photos, with arrows drawn from each photo to a spot on
the map.*

*He inspects the photos. Some are buildings, some are people. All have
handwritten notes on the broad white strip underneath the image.*

*Leonard takes Polaroids out of his pocket. The first one is of the Dis-
count Inn. He sticks it on to an already-squashed lump of blue tack at
the end of an arrow drawn from a location on the outskirts of town.*

*The second photo is a blurred shot of a brunette turning in a doorway.
The name* NATALIE *is written under the picture. Leonard flips it over.
On the back are two handwritten messages. The first one has been com-
pletely scribbled over, but the other one reads:*
'SHE HAS ALSO LOST SOMEONE, SHE WILL HELP YOU OUT OF
PITY'.

*Leonard nods, then sticks the photo to the chart. He steps back, looking
over the Polaroids one by one: Natalie, Burt, Discount Inn, Teddy.*

*He sits at the desk and opens the brown envelope. He takes out a
photocopy of a car registration and a driver's licence. Both are in the
name of John Edward Gammell, but when Leonard looks at the picture*

on the licence, he recognizes the face. Leonard moves back to his wall-chart, finds the Polaroid of Teddy and compares it to the licence photo.

> LEONARD (V.O.)
>
> This guy told me his name was Teddy.

He turns the photo over and examines the white strip on the back. It says only:
'DON'T BELIEVE HIS LIES'.

Leonard smiles. He goes to the phone and dials the number on the Polaroid. A couple of rings, then it's answered.

> TEDDY
>
> Yup?

> LEONARD
>
> Mr Gammell?

> TEDDY
>
> Lenny, is that you?

> LEONARD
>
> John Gammell?

> TEDDY
>
> Lenny, it's Teddy. Look, stay there, OK? I'm gonna be right over.

> LEONARD
>
> I'll be waiting.

He hangs up, thinking. He looks at the writing on the back of his hand, then pulls back his sleeve to reveal the words:
'THE FACTS:'.

He removes his jacket, then starts pulling off his shirt.

He has writing tattooed all over his chest, stomach and arms. Messages in different styles of writing, some crude, some elaborate. The messages run in all directions, some upside-down, some backwards. Leonard examines his tattoos, methodically. From Leonard's POV, the most striking is an upside-down tattoo on his belly which says:
'PHOTOGRAPH: HOUSE, CAR, FRIEND, FOE'.

On one forearm it says:
'THE FACTS:
FACT 1. MALE
FACT 2. WHITE'.

On the other forearm:
'FACT 3. FIRST NAME: JOHN OR JAMES
FACT 4. LAST NAME: G ___ '.

He pulls down his trousers. On his right thigh, crudely lettered:
'FACT 5. DRUG DEALER'.

And immediately below this, in elegant, neat lettering:
'FACT 6. CAR LICENSE NUMBER: SG13 7IU'.

Leonard takes out the registration document and examines it. Holding the photo of Teddy and the registration document, he checks off his tattooed facts:

> *(under his breath)*
> White . . . male. First name . . . John. Last name . . . G for
> Gammell. Drugs. Licence plate.
> *(checks document against tattoo on thigh)*
> SG . . . 13 . . . 7 . . . IU. It's him. It's actually him.

He looks coldly at Teddy's smiling image.

> I found you, you fuck.

He turns the photo face down, takes a pen and writes:
'HE IS THE ONE'.

He drops the pen. Thinks. He looks at his chest through the mirror and a backwards tattoo suddenly becomes clear:
'JOHN G. RAPED AND MURDERED MY WIFE'.

He buttons his blue shirt, then writes on the back of Teddy's picture:
'KILL HIM'.

He sticks the photo of Teddy between his teeth as he holds his handgun up and checks that it is loaded. He sticks the gun in the back of his waistband.

INT. MOTEL ROOM 21 – DAY [BLACK-AND-WHITE SEQUENCE]

Leonard, in his boxers and plaid work shirt, shaving foam on thigh, drops his disposable razor and cautiously picks up the ringing phone.

>   LEONARD
> Who is this?
>   (*listens*)

He unbuttons his shirt.

> And we spoke earlier? I don't remember that.
>   (*listens*)
> Well, yeah, but it's not amnesia. I remember *everything* from before my injury, I just can't make any new memories.
>   (*listens*)

He pulls his shirt off. There is a bandage on his left arm. He looks down at the tattoos all over his chest, stomach and arms.

> So I can't remember talking to you. What did we talk about?
>   (*nods*)
> Sammy Jankis. Yeah, I guess I tell people about Sammy to help them understand. Sammy's story helps me understand my own situation.

He touches the tattoo on the back of his hand.

> Sammy Jankis wrote himself endless notes. But he'd get mixed up. I've got a more graceful solution to the memory problem. I'm disciplined and organized. I use habit and routine to make my life possible. Sammy had no drive. No reason to make it work.

He can see his reflection in the mirror. He studies the tattoo across his chest:
'JOHN G. RAPED AND MURDERED MY WIFE'.

> Me? I gotta reason.

EXT. CITY GRILL ON MAIN STREET – DAY [COLOUR SEQUENCE]

Leonard parks the Jaguar, gets out, and stops outside the door to a restaurant, checking its name against a note written on a small paper bag from a pharmacy. The note says:

'CITY GRILL, MAIN ST. THURSDAY, I.OOPM MEET NATALIE FOR INFO'.

He sticks the note in his pocket and pulls out his Polaroid photographs. He flips through them until he finds Natalie's. Leonard flips the picture over. On the back are two handwritten messages. The first one has been completely scribbled over, the second reads:

'SHE HAS ALSO LOST SOMEONE, SHE WILL HELP YOU OUT OF PITY'.

INT. CITY GRILL ON MAIN STREET – DAY

Leonard enters, walking slowly down the aisle, looking at all the customers. He makes eye contact with a woman (brunette, 30s) sitting alone, wearing sunglasses. Her face betrays nothing. Leonard walks past. She sighs and grabs the back of his jacket as he passes. He spins around.

LEONARD

Natalie.

He slips into the seat opposite her. Natalie is pretty, but has bruising around one eye and a mark on her lip.

NATALIE

You don't remember me.

LEONARD
(friendly smile)

Sorry, I should have explained. You see, I have this condition –

NATALIE

You did explain, Lenny.

Leonard shifts uncomfortably.

LEONARD

Please call me Leonard. My wife called me Lenny.

NATALIE

You told me.

Leonard raises his eyebrows, then smiles.

> LEONARD
>
> Then I probably told you how much I hated it. Could you take off your sunglasses? It's just hard for me –

Natalie takes them off to reveal her bruises.

> NATALIE
>
> Yeah.

> LEONARD
>
> So you have information for me?

> NATALIE
>
> Is that what your little note says?

> LEONARD
>
> Yes.

> NATALIE
>
> Must be tough living life according to a few scraps of paper. Mix up your laundry list and your grocery list, you'll be eating your underwear.

She smiles.

> But I guess that's why you got those freaky tattoos.

Leonard is surprised.

> LEONARD
>
> It is tough. Almost impossible. I'm sorry I can't remember you. It's not personal.

Natalie's smile fades.

> NATALIE
>
> I'm sorry.

She takes a brown envelope out of her handbag.

> I do have information for you. You gave me a licence-plate number? I had my friend at the DMV trace it. Guess what name came up.

Leonard shrugs.

John Edward Gammell. John G.

LEONARD

You know him?

NATALIE

No. But the photo on his licence looked familiar. I think he's been in the bar before.

She slides the envelope towards him, but stops short.

This is a copy of his registration, licence, photo and all. Are you sure you want this?

LEONARD

Have I told you what this man did?

NATALIE

Yes.

LEONARD

Then you shouldn't have to ask.

NATALIE

But even if you get your revenge, you won't remember it. You won't even know it's happened.

LEONARD
(*annoyed*)

So I'll take a picture, get a tattoo.
(*calms*)

The world doesn't disappear when you close your eyes, does it? My actions still have meaning, even if I can't remember them. My wife deserves vengeance, and it doesn't make any difference whether I know about it.

NATALIE

Tell me about her again.

LEONARD

Why?

NATALIE

Because you like to remember her. I want to see you enjoy yourself.

LEONARD

She was beautiful. Perfect to me –

NATALIE

Don't just recite the words. Close your eyes, remember her.

Leonard smiles and shuts his eyes.

INSERT FLASHBACK:

INT. LEONARD'S APARTMENT – DAY

Random images of a woman (30s, black hair, plain). Jump cuts of details: a smile, eating, tucking her hair behind her ear, pulling on a pair of trousers, watching TV, shouting in anger. Sitting on the edge of the bed in her underwear, she turns as Leonard pinches her thigh.

LEONARD (V.O.)

You can only feel details. Bits and pieces which you didn't bother to put into words. And extreme moments you feel even if you don't want to. Put it together and you get the feel of the person, enough to know how much you miss them, and how much you hate the person who took them away.

INT. CITY GRILL – DAY

Leonard opens his eyes. Natalie is looking at him. She nods and hands him the brown envelope.

NATALIE

I wrote an address in there, too. Might be useful. It's this abandoned place outside of town. A guy I knew used to use it for his bigger deals.

LEONARD

Deals?

NATALIE

It's isolated.

LEONARD

Sounds perfect. What do I owe you?

                           NATALIE
I wasn't helping you for money.

                           LEONARD
Sorry.

                           NATALIE
It's not your fault. See, you have this condition . . .

Leonard smiles. Natalie reaches into her purse and pulls out a motel-room key.

Are you still at the Discount Inn? Room 304? You left this at my place.

Leonard pulls out a Polaroid of the Discount Inn.

                           LEONARD
The Discount Inn, yeah.

Natalie leaves the key and gets up from the table.

                           NATALIE
They treating you all right?

                           LEONARD
                          (*smiling*)
Don't remember.

                           NATALIE
You know what we have in common?

Leonard shrugs.

We're both survivors. Take care, Leonard.

Leonard watches Natalie leave. He sits at the table, looking down at the brown envelope and the motel-room key (room 304). He rises and heads to the restroom.

INT. RESTAURANT RESTROOM – DAY

Leonard flushes the urinal, then moves to the sink and starts washing his hands. He notices a message written on the back of his hand: 'REMEMBER SAMMY JANKIS'.

He stares at the message for a second, thoughtful, then tries to scrub the writing off his skin. To his surprise, it is indelible. Leonard looks at it, quizzical, then notices some markings on his wrist, pulling his sleeve back to get a better look. He can read the start of a message:
'THE FACTS:'.

Leonard is about to roll his sleeve up further when the restroom door opens and a man enters. Leonard dries his hands, then exits the restroom.

INT. MOTEL ROOM 21 – DAY [BLACK-AND-WHITE SEQUENCE]

Leonard (in boxers, bandaged arm) talks on the phone. He resumes shaving his thigh.

> LEONARD
> I met Sammy through work.
> (*listens*)
> Insurance. I was an *investigator*. I'd investigate claims to see which ones were phony.

He dips the razor into the steaming ice bucket.

> I had to see through people's bullshit. It was useful experience, because now it's my life. When I meet someone, I don't even know if I've met them before. I have to look in their eyes and just figure them out. My job taught me that the best way to find out what someone knew was to let them talk.

INT. LEONARD'S OFFICE – DAY

Montage: Leonard, wearing a cheap dark suit and tie, sitting opposite various different people in an interview situation.

> LEONARD (V.O.)
> Throw in the occasional 'Why?', but just listen. And watch the eyes, the body language.

He watches the people's movements carefully. We see close-ups of fiddling hands, neck scratching, etc.

> It's complicated. You might catch a sign but attach the wrong meaning to it. If someone touches their nose while they're talking, experts will tell you it means they're lying. It really

127

means they're nervous, and people get nervous for all sorts of reasons. It's all about context.

INT. MOTEL ROOM 21 — DAY

LEONARD

I was good. Sammy was my first real challenge.

EXT. DISCOUNT INN — DAY [COLOUR SEQUENCE]

The Jaguar pulls up. Leonard gets out and heads to the office.

INT. DISCOUNT INN OFFICE — DAY

Burt is behind the counter reading a magazine.

LEONARD

I'm sorry, I think I'm checked in here, but I've misplaced my key.

BURT
(looks up)

Hi, Leonard.

He puts his magazine down and gets up, sighing.

Probably in the room.

EXT. DISCOUNT INN — DAY

Burt, swinging a pass key on a chain, leads Leonard along the ground floor to room 21, and then unlocks it.

INT. DISCOUNT INN ROOM 21 — DAY

Leonard enters and scans the room. Burt picks his nails in the doorway. Leonard moves to the unmade bed. There is a pile of bloodstained tissues. On the bedside table is an ice bucket. Next to it is a disposable razor and a can of shaving foam.

LEONARD

I don't see my key.

Burt looks up. He realizes something.

BURT

Shit. Wrong room.

LEONARD

What?

Burt tries to shepherd Leonard out of the room.

BURT

This isn't your room. You're in 304. I fucked up.

LEONARD

This isn't my room?

BURT

No, let's go.

LEONARD

Then why is this my handwriting?

He picks a white paper bag up off the floor. Handwritten on the side is a message:
'SHAVE THIGH'.

Better tell me what the fuck's going on.

Burt looks uncomfortable.

BURT

This was your room. You're up in 304 now.

LEONARD

When was I in here?

BURT

Last week. Then I rented you another one on top of this.

LEONARD

Why?

BURT

Business is slow. I told my boss about you, about your condition. He told me to try and rent you another room.

LEONARD

Why didn't you clean it out?

                              BURT
                           (*shrugs*)
     You're still paying for it. It's still your room.

Leonard shakes his head, smiling.

                            LEONARD
     So how many rooms am I checked into in this dump?

                              BURT
     Just two. So far.

Leonard walks out past Burt.

                            LEONARD
     Well, at least you're being honest about cheating me.

                              BURT
     Yeah, well, you're not gonna remember, anyway.

                            LEONARD
     You don't have to be *that* honest, Burt.

                              BURT
     Leonard.

Leonard turns. Burt grins.

     Always get a receipt.

                            LEONARD
     I'm gonna write that down.

*Leonard fishes a piece of paper out of his pocket. There is a message on
it which he reads. It says:*
'CITY GRILL, MAIN ST. THURSDAY, I.OOPM MEET NATALIE FOR
INFO'.

Leonard looks up at Burt.

     What time is it?

EXT. ROAD — DAY

The Jaguar speeds along.

                              130

EXT. CITY GRILL ON MAIN STREET – DAY

Leonard checks the restaurant name against the note. He gets out his Polaroids, flipping through them until he finds the one of Natalie.

INT. CITY GRILL ON MAIN STREET – DAY

Leonard walks through the restaurant, checking the patrons. He makes eye contact with Natalie, but walks past her table. She sighs and grabs the back of his jacket.

CUT TO:

INT. MOTEL ROOM 21 – DAY [BLACK-AND-WHITE SEQUENCE]

Leonard (in boxers, bandaged arm) shaves his thigh, talking on the phone.

LEONARD
I'd just become an investigator when I came across Sammy. Mr Samuel R. Jankis – strangest case ever. Guy's fifty-eight, semi-retired accountant. He and his wife had been in this car accident . . . nothing too serious, but he's acting funny – he can't get a handle on what's going on.

INT. DOCTOR'S OFFICE – DAY

A doctor examines Sammy's head. Sammy's wife looks on.

LEONARD (V.O.)
The doctors find some possible damage to the hippocampus, nothing conclusive. But Sammy can't remember anything for more than a couple of minutes. He can't work, can't do shit, medical bills pile up, his wife calls the insurance company and I get sent in.

INT. JANKIS HOUSE – MESSY SUBURBAN LIVING ROOM – DAY

Sammy sits smoking, smiling at Leonard, who's wearing a cheap suit and tie.

LEONARD (V.O.)
My first big claims investigation – I really check into it. Sammy

131

can think just fine, but he can't make any new memories; he can only remember things for a few minutes.

Sammy watches a commercial on TV.

He'd watch TV, but anything longer than a couple of minutes was too confusing; he couldn't remember how it began. He liked commercials. They were short.

Sammy rolls a small glass bottle between the palms of his hands. Mrs Jankis rolls up her sleeve. Leonard watches as Sammy takes a syringe and pushes the needle through the rubber of the bottle. The label is marked 'INSULIN'.

The crazy part was that this guy who couldn't follow the plot of *Green Acres* could do the most complicated things as long as he had learned them before the accident . . .

Sammy inverts the bottle and syringe, draws the insulin into the syringe, withdraws the needle, holds it up to check for bubbles, tapping it delicately.

. . . and as long as he kept his mind on what he was doing.

Sammy wipes a spot on Mrs Jankis's arm with a swab, then gently pinches the skin and confidently inserts the needle. Mrs Jankis winces.

MRS JANKIS
Gentle.

Sammy looks up, worried. Mrs Jankis smiles at him. Sammy pushes the plunger, withdraws the needle and presses the swab against the skin, looking into Mrs Jankis's eyes and smiling back.

INT. JANKIS HOUSE FRONT HALL — DAY

Mrs Jankis opens the front door to Leonard. Leonard shakes hands with Sammy, who smiles at him in apparent recognition.

LEONARD (V.O.)
The doctors assure me that there's a real condition called Korsokoff's syndrome; short-term memory loss, rare but legit. But every time I see him I catch a look of recognition. Just a slight

132

look, but he says he can't remember me at all. I can read people and I'm thinking bad actor. Now I'm suspicious and I order more tests.

CUT TO:

INT. MOTEL ROOM 21 – DAY

Leonard dabs at some blood on his thigh with toilet paper.

> LEONARD
> His wife has to do everything. Sammy can only do simple stuff. He couldn't pick up any new skills at all, and that's how I got him.

EXT. MAIN STREET – DAY [COLOUR SEQUENCE]

Leonard's Jaguar pulls up at a red light. Suddenly Teddy is banging on the window.

> TEDDY
> Lenny! I thought you'd gone for good. What brings you back?

Leonard looks at Teddy, sizing him up.

> LEONARD
> Unfinished business. What made you think I wasn't coming back?

> TEDDY
> You said you were leaving town.

> LEONARD
> Things change.

> TEDDY
> So I see. It's good to see you. My name's Teddy.

> LEONARD
> Guess I've told you about my condition.

> TEDDY
> *(grins)*
> Only every time I see ya! Come on, I'll buy you lunch.

INT. DINER – DAY

Teddy pours ketchup all over his steak. Leonard plays with his food.

> TEDDY

Not hungry?

> LEONARD
> (*shrugs*)

It's my condition. I never know if I've already eaten, so I always just eat small amounts.

> TEDDY

You don't have to remember to be hungry.

> LEONARD

It's weird, but if you don't eat for a while then your body stops being hungry. You get sort of shaky but you don't realize you haven't eaten. Have I told you about Sammy Jankis?

> TEDDY

Yeah, yeah. I heard enough about him. Tell me about John G. You still think he's here, right?

> LEONARD

Who?

> TEDDY

The guy you're looking for, Johnny G. That's why you haven't left. Am I right?

Leonard shrugs. Teddy licks his fingers and frowns.

Leonard, you need to be very careful.

> LEONARD

Why?

> TEDDY

Well, the other day you made it sound like you thought somebody might be trying to set you up. Get you to kill the wrong guy.

> LEONARD

Yeah, well, I go on facts, not recommendations, OK?

TEDDY

Lenny, you can't trust a man's life to your little notes and pictures.

LEONARD

Why?

TEDDY

Because you're relying on them alone. You don't remember what you've discovered or how. Your notes might be unreliable.

LEONARD

Memory's unreliable.

Teddy snorts.

No, really. Memory's not perfect. It's not even that good. Ask the police; eyewitness testimony is unreliable. The cops don't catch a killer by sitting around remembering stuff. They collect facts, make notes, draw conclusions. Facts, not memories: that's how you investigate. I know, it's what I used to do. Memory can change the shape of a room or the colour of a car. It's an interpretation, not a record. Memories can be changed or distorted and they're irrelevant if you have the facts.

TEDDY

You really wanna find this guy?

LEONARD

He took away the woman I love and he took away my memory. He destroyed everything; my life and my ability to live.

TEDDY

You're living.

LEONARD

Just for revenge. That's what keeps me going. It's all I have.

Teddy considers this.

TEDDY

We'll find him. Where are you staying?

Leonard reaches into his pocket and takes out a Polaroid.

> LEONARD
> Discount Inn. Don't know what room, haven't got my key.

> TEDDY
> Probably left it in your room.

EXT. DISCOUNT INN — DAY

The Jaguar pulls up. Leonard gets out and heads to the office.

INT. DISCOUNT INN OFFICE — DAY

Leonard enters. Burt is behind the counter reading a magazine.

> LEONARD
> I'm sorry, I think I'm checked in here, but I've misplaced my key.

> BURT
> *(looks up)*
> Hi, Leonard.

INT. MOTEL ROOM 21 — DAY [BLACK-AND-WHITE SEQUENCE]

Leonard (in boxers, bandaged arm), shaving foam on thigh, strides the room, talking on the phone and gesticulating with a disposable razor.

> LEONARD
> So Sammy can't learn any new skills. But I find something in my research: conditioning. Sammy should still be able to learn through repetition. It's how you learn stuff like riding a bike, things you don't think about, you just get better through practice. Call it muscle memory, whatever, but it's a completely different part of the brain from the short-term memory. So I have the doctors test Sammy's response to conditioning . . .

INT. EXAMINATION ROOM — DAY

Sammy sits at a table. A Doctor sits opposite pointing out various metal objects sitting on the table.

> DOCTOR

Just pick up any three objects.

> SAMMY
> (amused)

That's a test? Where were you guys when I did my CPA?

Sammy picks up an object and gestures to the Doctor for applause. Sammy goes for a second object, but gets a shock which makes him recoil in pain.

Ah! What the fuck?!

He looks accusingly at the Doctor.

> DOCTOR

It's a test, Sammy.

> LEONARD (V.O.)

Some of the objects were electrified; they'd give him a small shock.

INT. MOTEL ROOM 21 — DAY

> LEONARD

They kept repeating the test, always with the same objects electrified. The point was to see if he could learn to avoid the electrified objects. Not by memory, but by instinct.

INT. NATALIE'S BEDROOM: MESSY, CHEAPLY BUT ABUNDANTLY FURNISHED — MORNING [COLOUR SEQUENCE]

Leonard opens his eyes, naked in bed. He looks around, confused. With a start, he realizes that someone else is in the bed: a brunette with her back to him.

He leans right over her to get a look at her face. It is Natalie. The bruise on her eye and the mark on her lip are worse than before.

She opens her eyes and is startled by the sight of Leonard's hovering face.

> LEONARD

Sorry. It's only me.

He flops down. Natalie wakes up fully and relaxes.

NATALIE

Sleep OK?

LEONARD

Yeah. You?

Natalie shrugs. She looks at her bedside clock.

NATALIE

I gotta be someplace.

She gets out of bed, wearing pyjamas. Leonard swings his legs out of the bed and realizes that he is wearing trousers and socks. He looks at his tattoos, as if he has never seen them before.

Pretty weird.

She is smiling at him in the mirror. Leonard smiles, shrugs.

LEONARD

Useful. You never write a phone number on your hand?

NATALIE
(*through mirror*)

I should be able to talk to my friend about the licence plate today.

LEONARD

Yeah, the licence plate . . .

NATALIE
(*smiles*)

John G.'s licence-plate number. You have it tattooed on your thigh.

She leaves the room. Leonard pulls down his trousers to reveal two tattoos:
'FACT 5: DRUG DEALER'
'FACT 6: CAR LICENSE NUMBER: SG13 7IU'.

Leonard runs his finger over Fact 6, then pulls his trousers up and looks around the room. He spots his suit jacket hanging over the back of a chair. He checks the pockets, pulls out his Polaroids, flips through them:

a Jaguar, the Discount Inn, Natalie. He flips Natalie's picture over and looks at the back. There are two messages, but the first one has been completely scribbled over. The other one reads:
'SHE HAS ALSO LOST SOMEONE, SHE WILL HELP YOU OUT OF PITY'.

He stuffs the photos back into his pocket, grabs a white shirt off the chair and pulls it on. Natalie comes back in and starts to apply her make-up.

If it's registered in this state it'll just take seconds to pull up his licence and registration. I'll call when I've spoken to him.

LEONARD

Why don't we just arrange a meeting now? I'm not too good on the phone.

Natalie takes her eye pencil and writes a note on a small bag from a pharmacy. Leonard puts his jacket on. Natalie offers him the note. It says:
'CITY GRILL, MAIN ST. THURSDAY, 1.00PM MEET NATALIE FOR INFO'.

(*reading*)

It's great that you would . . . that you're helping me like this . . .

NATALIE
(*smiles*)

I'm helping you because you helped me.

Leonard nods.

So will you remember me next time you see me?

Leonard shakes his head and reaches for the note. Natalie grabs his lapel and pulls him down to her, kissing him gently on the mouth.

I think you will.

LEONARD
(*smiles*)

I'm sorry.

He heads for the door.

                    NATALIE
                    (*amused*)
Lenny, before you go, can I have my shirt back please?

*She tosses him his blue shirt. Leonard looks down at the white shirt
which he has put on. It is way too small.*

EXT. MAIN STREET − DAY

*The Jaguar pulls up at a red light. Suddenly Teddy is banging on the
window.*

                    TEDDY
Lenny! I thought you'd gone for good. What brings you
back?

INT. MOTEL ROOM 21 − DAY [BLACK-AND-WHITE SEQUENCE]

*Leonard (in boxers, bandaged arm) strides the room, shaving foam
on leg, razor in one hand, phone in the other.*

                    LEONARD
They kept testing Sammy for months, always with the same
objects carrying the electrical charge . . .

INT. EXAMINATION ROOM − DAY

*Sammy sits across the testing table from the Doctor. Sammy goes
for a metal object and recoils in pain from a shock.*

                    SAMMY
Ah! What the fuck?!

                    DOCTOR
It's a test, Sammy.

JUMP CUT TO:

INT. EXAMINATION ROOM − DAY

*As before, but Sammy is dressed differently. He goes for an object
and is shocked.*

SAMMY

Ah! What the fuck?!

DOCTOR

It's a test, Sammy.

Sammy extends a trembling middle finger.

SAMMY

Yeah? Test this, you fucking quack.

Sequence of jump cuts of Sammy extending his middle finger and recoiling in shock from the objects.

LEONARD (V.O.)

Even with total short-term memory loss, Sammy should've learned to instinctively stop picking up the wrong objects. All previous cases of short-term memory loss had responded to conditioning in some way. Sammy didn't respond at all.

INT. MOTEL ROOM 21 — DAY

LEONARD

It was enough to suggest his condition was psychological, not physical. We turned down his claim on the grounds that he wasn't covered for mental illness. Sammy's wife got stuck with the bills and I got a promotion for rejecting a big claim.

He looks into the mirror.

Conditioning didn't work for Sammy, so he became helpless. But it works for me. I live the way Sammy couldn't. Habit and routine makes my life possible. Conditioning. Acting on instinct.

EXT./INT. NATALIE'S FRONT DOOR — DUSK [COLOUR SEQUENCE]

Leonard pulls up in his Jaguar, gets out, rings the front doorbell. It is opened by Natalie.

LEONARD

Natalie, right?

Natalie nods, wary of Leonard's barely concealed anger. Leonard thrusts a Polaroid in her face.

Who the fuck is Dodd?

The photo is of a man who is bound, gagged and bloody. On the back of the photo:
'GET RID OF HIM, ASK NATALIE'.

Natalie takes the picture and examines it.

NATALIE
Guess I don't have to worry about him any more.

LEONARD
(*snaps*)
Who is he?! What have you got me into?!

Natalie looks up and down the street.

NATALIE

Come inside.

INT. NATALIE'S LIVING ROOM: COMFORTABLE AND MESSY — NIGHT

Natalie shows Leonard in.

NATALIE
Calm down. You're not into anything. It was my problem, you offered to help. It's got nothing to do with your investigation.

LEONARD
That's the problem! How can I find John G. when I don't know what's going on?! How did you get me into this?!

NATALIE
Leonard, you offered to help when you saw what this guy did to me.

She gestures at the bruising on her face.

LEONARD
How do I know he did that to you?

NATALIE

I came to you straight after he did it. I showed you what he'd
done and asked for your help.

LEONARD

So I just take your word?

NATALIE

Yes.

LEONARD
(*sighs*)
Something feels wrong. I think someone's fucking with me.
Trying to get me to kill the wrong guy.

NATALIE

Did you?

LEONARD

What?

NATALIE

Kill him.

LEONARD

Course not.

Natalie waves the Polaroid at him.

NATALIE

This has nothing to do with you. You helped me out, and I'm
grateful.

*She tries to rip the picture. Leonard watches her try. The plastic is too
strong.*

LEONARD

You have to burn them.

*Natalie scrunches it up and throws it down. Leonard and Natalie sit
down on the couch.*

NATALIE

You decided to help me. Trust yourself. Trust your own

judgment. You can question everything, you can never know anything for sure.

LEONARD

There are things you know for sure.

NATALIE

Such as?

LEONARD

I know the feel of the world.
(*reaches forward*)
I know how this wood will sound when I knock.
(*raps knuckles on coffee table*)
I know how this glass will feel when I pick it up.
(*handles glass*)
Certainties. You think it's knowledge, but it's a kind of memory, a kind you take for granted. I can remember so much.
(*runs hand over objects*)
I know the feel of the world . . .
(*beat*)
. . . and I know her.

NATALIE

Your wife?

LEONARD

She's gone and the present is trivia, which I can scribble down as notes.

Natalie stares at Leonard, thinking.

NATALIE

Relax a little, OK? Take off your jacket.

Leonard takes his jacket off and places it on the back of the couch, patting the pockets as he does so.

LEONARD

It's not easy to be calm when –

NATALIE

Just relax.

144

She reaches for his arm and unbuttons his cuff, revealing the end of Leonard's tattoos.

You don't seem the type.

She pushes back the sleeve, trying to read the tattoo. Leonard watches her.

Come on.

She starts to unbutton his shirt. He watches. Natalie gasps as she opens Leonard's shirt and pulls it back over his shoulders. She tilts her head, trying to read the different messages.

It's backwards.

She pulls him up and turns him around in front of the mirror to read the backwards tattoo across his chest.
'JOHN G. RAPED AND MURDERED MY WIFE'.

She touches the blank area of skin above Leonard's heart.

Here?

Leonard looks down at the blank patch, then at Natalie, vulnerable, confused.

LEONARD
It's . . . it must be for when I've found him.

Natalie looks at him. He shrugs. She studies his chest, avoiding his eyes.

NATALIE
I've lost somebody.

LEONARD
I'm sorry.

Natalie picks up a photograph from a messy desk in the corner. She shows it to Leonard. The picture shows Natalie smiling and hugging a smirking young man (Jimmy). Natalie looks up at Leonard to see his reaction.

NATALIE
His name was Jimmy.

LEONARD

What happened?

NATALIE

He went to meet somebody and didn't come back.

LEONARD

Who did he go to meet?

Natalie studies Leonard.

NATALIE

A guy called Teddy.

Leonard does not react to the name.

LEONARD

What do the police think?

NATALIE

They don't look too hard for guys like Jimmy.

She puts the photo down. She reaches out to Leonard, spreading her fingers over the blank part of his chest.

When you find this guy, this John G., what are you going to do?

LEONARD

Kill him.

NATALIE

Maybe I can help you find him. I know a lot of people.

INT. NATALIE'S BEDROOM — NIGHT

Natalie, eyes closed, has her head on Leonard's chest. He is shirtless, lying on top of the covers.

LEONARD

I don't even know how long she's been gone. It's like I've woken up in bed and she's not here because she's gone to the bathroom or something. But somehow I just know that she'll never come back to bed. I lie here, not knowing how long I've been alone. If I could just reach out and touch her side

146

of the bed I could know that it was cold, but I can't. I have
no idea when she left.

Natalie's eyes are open.

I know I can't have her back, but I want to be able to let her
go. I don't want to wake up every morning thinking she's still
here then realizing that she's not. I want time to pass, but it
won't. How can I heal if I can't feel time?

*He bends his head around to see if Natalie is awake. She closes her
eyes. Leonard gingerly slides from underneath her and moves silently
out of the bedroom.*

INT. NATALIE'S LIVING ROOM – NIGHT

*Leonard enters the dark room. He goes to the couch and picks up his
shirt and his jacket. He notices the photograph which Natalie showed
him on top of some papers on a desk in the corner. He holds it in a
shaft of light from the streetlamp outside, studying the photo of Natalie
and Jimmy.*

INT. NATALIE'S BEDROOM – NIGHT

*Natalie, eyes open, slides her hand over to where Leonard was lying,
feeling his residual warmth.*

INT. NATALIE'S LIVING ROOM – NIGHT

*Leonard has his Polaroid photograph of Natalie out. He takes a pen
out of his jacket, rests the photo against the wall in a patch of light and
writes on the back, underneath the message which has been scribbled
out:*
'SHE HAS ALSO LOST SOMEONE, SHE WILL HELP YOU OUT OF
PITY'.

INT. NATALIE'S BEDROOM – NIGHT – CONTINUOUS

*Leonard enters, deposits his jacket and shirt, then slides into bed next to
Natalie.*

INT. MOTEL ROOM 21 – DAY [BLACK-AND-WHITE SEQUENCE]

Leonard lies on the bed (in boxers, bandaged arm) talking on the phone. He wipes the excess shaving foam from his thigh, and feels the smoothness of the clean-shaven skin.

LEONARD

Sammy's wife was crippled by the cost of supporting him and fighting the company's decision – but it wasn't the money that got to her.

INT. JANKIS HOUSE LIVING ROOM – DAY

Mrs Jankis comes into the room. Sammy is seated, watching TV. He looks up at her with a smile. She smiles back, tense.

LEONARD (V.O.)

I never said that Sammy was faking. Just that his problem was mental, not physical. But she . . . she couldn't understand. She looks into his eyes and sees the same person. And if it's not a physical problem . . .

Sammy's wife starts shouting at Sammy. Sammy squirms.

. . . he should just . . . snap out of it.

Sammy's wife throws her drink in Sammy's face, puts her head in her hands, sobbing. Sammy wipes his face on his sleeve.

INT. MOTEL ROOM 21 – DAY

Leonard, talking on the phone, empties the white paper bag on to the bed beside him: two cheap ball-point pens, scotch tape, a pack of needles and a file card.

LEONARD

So good old Leonard Shelby from the insurance company gives her the seed of doubt, just like he gave it to the doctors. But I never said that Sammy was faking. I never said that.

He takes a needle out of the packet.

INT. LEONARD'S APARTMENT WITH HIGH CEILINGS AND WOODEN
FLOORS – NIGHT [COLOUR SEQUENCE]

*We move along a hallway towards a closed door. An ominous rumbling
builds.*

INSERT QUICK CUTS:

Trembling, shallow-focus extreme close-ups:

*A glass bottle shatters against black-and-white ceramic tiles. A sudden
movement glimpsed through a water-beaded clear plastic shower curtain.*

The shower curtain pulls taut across a gasping female face.

Leonard's reflection in a mirror which shatters.

INT. DODD'S MOTEL ROOM – DAY

*Leonard opens his eyes, frightened. He is lying on the bed in his beige
suit and blue shirt.*

LEONARD (V.O.)

Awake.

He rolls his eyes to one side.

Where am I?

He lifts his head and surveys the room.

Motel room.

*He rises from the bed, looking at the room as if for the first time. He
starts looking in the dresser drawers, finding nothing.*

Some anonymous motel room. Nothing in the drawers, but
you look anyway.

He grasps the handle of the bedside drawer.

Never anything but the Gideon . . .

He pulls the drawer open, and pauses at what he sees.

. . . Bible.

In the drawer is a Gideon Bible. Resting on top of it is a handgun.

Leonard turns, looks over the rest of the room. He moves to the bureau and opens drawers. Empty. He goes to the closet and opens it.

Inside is a bound and gagged Man on the floor, knees against chest. His mouth is taped up with silver electrical tape, stained with dried blood from his swollen nose. He looks up at Leonard, blinking in the sudden bright light, terrified.

Leonard shuts the closet door, confused. The Man in the closet starts grunting and bumping the closet door.

There is a knock at the door. Leonard looks through the peephole.

INT./EXT. DODD'S MOTEL – DAY

    INSERT LEONARD'S POV:

A fish-eye Teddy, grinning and waving.

INT. DODD'S MOTEL – DAY

Leonard looks around, trying to think. Teddy knocks harder. The Man in the closet bumps and groans. Leonard reaches into his pocket and pulls out some Polaroids.

                   LEONARD
  Just a minute!

He finds the one of Teddy, then sticks them back into his pocket. He opens the door to Teddy and grins.

  Teddy!

Teddy brushes past him into the room.

                   TEDDY
  Finished playing with yourself, Lenny?

He slumps into a chair. Leonard tries to smile. There is a faint grunting and bumping from inside the closet. Teddy notices the noise and grins.

  I get it – amorous neighbours.

                   LEONARD
  Why are you here?

TEDDY
(*surprised*)

You called me. You wanted my help. You know, Lenny, I've had more rewarding friendships than this one. Although I do get to keep using the same jokes.

Leonard thinks, then moves to the closet and opens the door. Teddy looks in disbelief at the Man in the closet.

Who the fuck is that?

LEONARD

You don't know him?

TEDDY

No! Should I?

Leonard shrugs.

Is this John G.?

LEONARD

I don't think so.

TEDDY

Think so? You don't know? Didn't you write it down?

LEONARD

I might have fallen asleep before I did.

Teddy shakes his head, chuckling.

TEDDY

Ask him.

Leonard crouches down and rips the tape from the Man's mouth.

LEONARD

What's your name?

The Man looks at Leonard, wary, says nothing. Leonard tweaks his broken nose. The Man groans.

Your name.

MAN

Dodd.

LEONARD

Who did this to you?

DODD
(*confused*)

What?

LEONARD

Who did this to you?

DODD

You did.

Leonard replaces the gag and shuts the closet.

TEDDY

I'm not gonna help you kill this guy, if that's what –

LEONARD

No. No, just let me think for a minute.

He moves to the dresser and starts methodically emptying his pockets. He pulls a Polaroid out of his inside jacket pocket.

Here we go.

The Polaroid shows Dodd sitting on the bed, bound, gagged and bleeding. The name 'DODD' is written below the picture. Leonard flips it over. On the back it says:
'GET RID OF HIM, ASK NATALIE'.

Teddy looks at the photo over Leonard's shoulder.

TEDDY

Natalie? Natalie who?

LEONARD

Why?

TEDDY

I think I know her.

Leonard sticks the pictures in his pocket.

LEONARD

We've got to get him out of here.

TEDDY

He's got to have a car, right? We just take him back to his car and tell him to get the fuck out of town before we kill him.

LEONARD

We can't just walk him out tied up and bleeding.

TEDDY

How'd ya get him in here in the first place?

LEONARD

I don't know.

He looks around the room for inspiration.

Yes I do . . . this isn't my room.

Teddy looks around at the anonymous room.

It's his. He was already here. Let's just go.

He starts for the door. Teddy lays a hand on his chest.

TEDDY

Wait, we can't just leave him. The maid finds him, calls the cops. He's seen us now.

Leonard thinks.

LEONARD

OK. We clean him up, untie him and march him out with a gun in his back.

TEDDY

Why would I have a gun?

Leonard fishes the handgun out of the bedside-table drawer.

LEONARD

It must be his. I don't think they'd let someone like me carry a gun.

TEDDY

Fucking hope not.

Leonard covers Dodd with the gun while Teddy pulls him out of the closet. Dodd has trouble standing up straight.

EXT. DODD'S MOTEL — DAY

Teddy exits the room, glances around, motions for Leonard and Dodd to follow. Dodd is cleaned up and unbound, Leonard is pressed up right behind him. The three of them descend to the parking lot.

> LEONARD

Which one?

Dodd leads them to a new Landcruiser. Teddy whispers in Leonard's ear.

> TEDDY

We probably ought to take his car, you know, teach him a lesson.

> LEONARD

Shut it, Teddy.

> TEDDY

Easy for you to say, you've got the Jag.

> LEONARD

I'll ride with him. You follow.

> TEDDY

Give me your keys.

Leonard looks at him, suspicious.

> LEONARD

Take your own car.

Teddy shrugs. Leonard motions Dodd into the driver's seat, then slides into the passenger side. They pull out of the parking lot, Teddy following in his grey sedan.

EXT. SHOULDER OF HIGHWAY HEADING OUT OF TOWN — DAY

The Landcruiser pulls over and stops. The grey sedan pulls up behind. Leonard gets out of the Landcruiser and it pulls away at speed. He walks back to Teddy's car.

INT. GREY SEDAN – DAY

> **TEDDY**
> So was he scared?

> **LEONARD**
> Yeah. I think it was your sinister mustache that got him.

Teddy leans over slightly so that he can see his reflection in the rear-view mirror. Leonard smiles. Teddy sees him.

> **TEDDY**
> Fuck you. We shoulda taken his car.

> **LEONARD**
> What's wrong with this one?

> **TEDDY**
> You like it? Let's trade.

EXT. ALLEY BEHIND THE MOTEL – DAY

The grey sedan pulls up beside Leonard's Jaguar. Leonard gets out.

> **TEDDY**
> So what are you gonna do now?

> **LEONARD**
> I'm gonna ask Natalie what the fuck that was all about.

> **TEDDY**
> Natalie who?

Leonard ignores him and gets into his Jaguar.

EXT. MODEST SINGLE-STOREY HOUSE – NATALIE'S – DUSK

The Jaguar pulls up. Leonard checks the address against the address written on his Polaroid of Natalie, then goes to the door and rings the bell. It is opened by Natalie.

> **LEONARD**
> Natalie, right?

Natalie nods, wary of Leonard's tone. He thrusts a Polaroid in her face.

Who the fuck is Dodd?

The photo shows Dodd, bound, gagged and bleeding.

CUT TO:

INT. MOTEL ROOM 21 – DAY [BLACK-AND-WHITE SEQUENCE]

Leonard (boxers, bandaged arm) talks on the phone as he takes a needle and tapes it to the ball-point pen.

> LEONARD
> What Mrs Jankis didn't understand was that you can't bully someone into remembering . . . the more pressure you're under, the harder it gets.
> > (*listens*)
> Then call me back.

He hangs up.

INT. BATHROOM OF DODD'S MOTEL ROOM – DAY [COLOUR SEQUENCE]

Leonard sits on the toilet, grasping an empty vodka bottle by the neck. He notices the bottle in his hands as if for the first time.

> LEONARD (V.O.)
> Don't feel drunk.

He looks up from the vodka bottle, sighs, rubs his face, then stands up. He sniffs at his armpit.

He puts the empty bottle on the counter by the sink, then wearily undresses.

Leonard, naked, looks in the mirror, then runs the shower and steps under it, shutting the pebbled plastic stall door.

He showers. He turns the water off, then hears the door being unlocked. He freezes, standing in the shower stall, naked and dripping. Through the distortion of the pebbled plastic door he sees a figure enter the bathroom and start pissing into the toilet. The distorted figure turns and approaches the shower stall, becoming clearer as it gets closer, then yanks the door open. It is Dodd (without injuries). He is shocked to see

156

the naked Leonard. Leonard bursts out of the shower stall, smashing Dodd against the wall.

Dodd struggles around, grabbing at the slippery, naked Leonard. He pushes against Leonard, slamming him into the sink.

Leonard has his arms around Dodd's neck. He smashes Dodd's head sideways into the wall, hard.

Dodd slumps to the floor. Leonard exhales. Dodd puts a fist in Leonard's crotch, then grabs his neck as he doubles over. He uses Leonard to pull himself off the floor, then punches the side of his head and pushes him hard. Leonard flails wildly, grabbing the empty vodka bottle from by the sink as he falls back into the bedroom. Dodd reaches into his inside pocket.

INT. DODD'S MOTEL ROOM — DAY

Leonard stumbles in, naked, from the bathroom, swings around, hitting Dodd square in the face with the empty vodka bottle, which does not break.

Dodd lies motionless on the floor, bleeding, his hand still in his inside jacket pocket. Leonard stands above him, naked, dripping wet, catching his breath.

There is a knock at the door.

> FEMALE VOICE (O.S.)
Housekeeping.

The sound of a key entering the lock. Leonard leaps for the door and flips the privacy latch.

> LEONARD
Not just now!

He listens to the maid withdraw her key. Leonard searches Dodd, finding his gun in his inside pocket. He examines the weapon, then starts to search the room. He finds an overnight bag at the bottom of the closet. Inside it there are some clothes, spare ammunition, a large hunting knife and a roll of silver electrical tape.

He wraps the electrical tape around Dodd's wrists, then across his mouth. He finishes taping up Dodd, then sits him on the edge of the bed. He takes a Polaroid photo of the bloody, taped-up Dodd.

Leonard shoves Dodd into the closet, takes out a note and consults it, then writes 'DODD' on the white strip on the front of the photograph. He flips the picture over and writes on the strip on the back, in smaller writing: 'GET RID OF HIM, ASK NATALIE'.

He dresses, and puts the Polaroid into the inside pocket of his jacket. He looks again at the note. It says:
'DODD, MOUNTCREST INN ON 5TH STREET, ROOM 6
PUT HIM ON TO TEDDY OR JUST GET RID OF HIM FOR NATALIE'.

Leonard picks the stack of Polaroids out of his outside jacket pocket. He flips through them until he finds the one of Teddy, then picks up the phone and dials Teddy's number. The phone is answered.

> TEDDY (O.S.)
> You know what to do.

Then a beep. Leonard does not look like he knows what to do.

> LEONARD
> Ah, it's a message for Teddy . . .

He looks at the note.

> I'm at the Mountcrest Inn on 5th Street, room 6, and I need you to come over as soon as you get this. It's important. This is Leonard. Thanks. Bye.

He hangs up. He looks around the room. He slips the handgun into the bedside drawer, resting it on the Gideon Bible, then swings his feet up on to the bed and lies down.

> CUT TO:

INT. MOTEL ROOM 21 – DAY [BLACK-AND-WHITE SEQUENCE]

Leonard (boxers, bandaged arm) crooks his neck to hold the phone. In his hands is the pen with the needle taped to it.

He wiggles the needle, then applies more tape.

> CUT TO:

INT. MOTEL ROOM 21 – DAY

Leonard (boxers, bandaged arm) takes the needle/pen in one hand and picks up a cigarette lighter in the other.

He ignites the lighter, then holds the needle over the flame.

He examines the needle, then holds it in the flame again.

He puts down the lighter and picks up a second ball-point pen.

EXT. DODD'S MOTEL – DAY [COLOUR SEQUENCE]

Leonard's Jaguar pulls up, fast. Several bits of shattered safety glass are still visible in the frame. He parks around the back, out of sight, and consults a note.

LEONARD (V.O.)
I'll get the jump on you, fucker.

He races up the stairs to the rooms on the second floor. He stops at room 9, listening. The TV is on.

He gets a credit card out and slips it into the lock gently, with a practiced hand. He leaves the card wedged in the lock, then steps back from the door and knocks.

He watches the point of light in the peephole to room 9.

The point of light goes out. Leonard kicks the door in, smashing the room's occupant back into the room.

Leonard stands over him, looking down. The man is unconscious, blood on his face. Something is not right.

Is this the guy?

He looks down at his note. The room number given is 6. Leonard looks at the '9' on the door, then down at the unconscious man.

Fuck! Sorry.

He reaches down, grabs his credit card from where it landed on the floor, and backs out of the doorway, shutting the door on the unconscious man.

He moves quickly to room 6, slips his credit card in the lock and knocks.

No answer, so he slips inside.

INT. DODD'S MOTEL ROOM — DAY

Leonard flicks the light on and glances around. There is nothing in the room except an empty vodka bottle on the bedside table.

> LEONARD (V.O.)
>
> Need a weapon.

He grabs the empty vodka bottle, switches the light off and slips into the bathroom.

INT. DODD'S MOTEL ROOM BATHROOM — DAY

Leonard sits down on the toilet, holding the empty bottle by its neck. He reaches out and adjusts the angle of the door. His eyes are alert, he is nervous. Waiting. And waiting.

INT. MOTEL ROOM 21 — DAY [BLACK-AND-WHITE SEQUENCE]

Leonard (boxers, bandaged arm), takes the second ball-point pen and snaps it in two.

EXT. SMALL ALLEY BEHIND A ROW OF TRAILER HOMES — DAY [COLOUR SEQUENCE]

Leonard is running furiously, arms pumping.

> LEONARD (V.O.)
>
> What the fuck am I doing?

He glances to his right, and through a gap between two trailers he catches a glimpse of Dodd on the other side of the trailer homes, racing along parallel to Leonard.

> Chasing him!

He cuts down the next gap between trailers, heading full speed for Dodd's side.

Dodd (without bruises) appears again at the other end of the gap, sees Leonard, and starts running towards him. There is a gun in his hand.

> FUCK! He's chasing me.

Leonard skids to a halt and turns around. A bullet hits the dirt by his feet. He clears the end of the trailer and throws himself over a chain-link fence, dropping down on the other side and scrambling through some bushes. He races full tilt into a parking lot, looking around, desperate. He can hear a car alarm sounding. He pulls his keys out and hits the alarm switch. Hearing the double beep as the alarm stops, he spots the Jaguar.

The Jaguar peels out just as Dodd emerges from the trailer park.

INT. JAGUAR – DAY

Leonard is breathing hard, looking around nervously. He starts knocking bits of broken window glass out of the driver's-side window with his elbow, then pulling photos and pieces of paper out of his pockets as he drives.

He finds a note that gives a description of Dodd, along with the motel and room number of where Dodd is staying.

    CUT TO:

INT. MOTEL ROOM 21 – DAY [BLACK-AND-WHITE SEQUENCE]

Leonard (boxers, bandaged arm) has the needle/pen in one hand and the broken pen in the other. He dips the needle into the clear plastic ink reservoir of the broken pen.

EXT. TRAILER PARK PARKING LOT – DAY [COLOUR SEQUENCE]

Leonard is in the Jaguar. Dodd (without any bruises) is standing by the window, aiming his gun at Leonard.

              DODD
I haven't made a strong enough impression.

            LEONARD
            (amused)
Don't be too hard on yourself.

Dodd motions for Leonard to open the passenger-side door.

He gets into the passenger seat, gun on Leonard. Leonard nods to him.

    Seat belt.

He starts to reach over his left shoulder with his right hand as if for the seat belt. Dodd watches Leonard's right hand.

With his left hand, Leonard opens the door. He rolls out, slamming the door in Dodd's face, and hitting the central locking on his car keys.

He takes off across the asphalt. Dodd tries the doors, then shoots at Leonard, shattering the driver's-side window, triggering the car alarm.

Dodd climbs through the window and takes off after him.

Leonard slips into a trailer park, tripping as he dives into a gap between two trailers, stumbling over the plastic lawn furniture and old bikes which litter the narrow gap.

He picks himself up and sprints into the alley behind the trailers. He races along behind them. He is running furiously, arms pumping.

> LEONARD (V.O.)
> What the fuck am I doing?

Leonard glances to his right, and through a gap between the two trailers he catches a glimpse of Dodd on the other side of the trailer homes, racing along parallel to Leonard.

> Chasing him!

He cuts down the next gap between trailers, heading full speed for Dodd's side.

> CUT TO:

INT. MOTEL ROOM 21 – DAY [BLACK-AND-WHITE SEQUENCE]

Leonard looks at the ink-covered needle. He consults the file card. It has a handwritten message:
'TATTOO: ACCESS TO DRUGS'.

> CUT TO:

EXT. ĐISCOUNT INN – NIGHT [COLOUR SEQUENCE]

Leonard exits room 304 of the Discount Inn carrying a shopping bag, looking grim-faced.

INT. JAGUAR — NIGHT

Leonard gets in, gently places the bag on the passenger seat.

EXT. STREET — NIGHT

The Jaguar speeds along.

EXT. PARKING LOT OVERLOOKING RESERVOIR — NIGHT

Leonard gets out of the Jaguar, carrying the shopping bag. He climbs the chain-link fence.

EXT. RESERVOIR — NIGHT

Leonard has built a small fire. He reaches into the bag and removes a small stuffed toy. He douses it with lighter fluid and places it on the fire. He watches the fur blacken and the plastic eyes melt.

He reaches into the bag and pulls out a well-worn paperback book, whose cover has long since been ripped off. Leonard flicks through the pages.

INT. BEDROOM, LEONARD'S APARTMENT — NIGHT

Leonard is undressing. Leonard's Wife is in bed, reading the well-worn paperback.

LEONARD

How can you read that again?

LEONARD'S WIFE
(without looking up)

It's good.

LEONARD

You've read it a hundred times.

LEONARD'S WIFE

I enjoy it.

LEONARD

Yeah, but the pleasure of a book is in wanting to know what happens next –

163

LEONARD'S WIFE
(*looks up, annoyed*)
Don't be a prick. I'm not reading it to annoy you. I enjoy it.
Just let me read, please.

EXT. RESERVOIR – NIGHT

*Leonard places the book on the fire. He reaches into the bag, produces a
bra and a hairbrush. He puts the bra on the fire, then pulls some black
hair out of the hairbrush. He holds a few strands out above the fire
until they shrivel up in the heat. He does this with a larger clump and
it produces a small flame, so he drops it into the fire.*

LEONARD (V.O.)
Probably tried this before. Probably burned truckloads of
your stuff. Can't remember to forget you.

*He drops the brush on to the fire, pulls a green alarm clock out of the
bag, and adds it to the fire. Once the bag is empty, Leonard places it on
the fire. He sits looking at the flames.*

DISSOLVE TO:

EXT. RESERVOIR – DAWN

The sky has brightened. Leonard kicks the dying embers apart.

INT./EXT. JAGUAR – DAWN

*The Jaguar speeds along. Leonard looks into his rear-view mirror to see
a Landcruiser following him. Leonard speeds up, turns right. The
Landcruiser sticks behind.*

LEONARD (V.O.)
Do I know this guy?

*He fishes photographs out of his pocket, examining them. The Land-
cruiser accelerates until it is uncomfortably close. Leonard slows, turning into a parking lot. The Landcruiser follows.*

He seems to know me.

*The Landcruiser pulls alongside the Jaguar. Leonard looks over. Dodd
(no bruises) is at the wheel. Leonard rolls down his window.*

What the fuck!

Dodd pulls out a handgun and points it at Leonard. Leonard slams on the brakes, jerking to a halt as the Landcruiser pulls over in front of the Jaguar.

EXT. TRAILER PARK PARKING LOT — DAY

Dodd, gun in hand, gets out of the Landcruiser and approaches.

> DODD
>
> I like your car.

> LEONARD
>
> Thanks.

> DODD
>
> Where'd you get it?

> LEONARD
>
> Interested in buying one?

> DODD
>
> I just want you to tell me how you came by that car.

> LEONARD
>
> I forget.

Dodd points his gun at Leonard through the window.

> DODD
>
> I haven't made a strong enough impression on you.

> LEONARD
> (*amused*)
> I wouldn't be too hard on yourself.

INT. MOTEL ROOM 21 — DAY [BLACK-AND-WHITE SEQUENCE]

Leonard (boxers, bandaged arm) drops the file card and pushes the ink-covered needle against his thigh, about to break the skin.

The phone rings, surprising him. He watches it ring, then reaches out with his bandaged arm to lift the receiver.

LEONARD

Who is this?

CUT TO:

INT. DISCOUNT INN ROOM 304 – NIGHT [COLOUR SEQUENCE]

Leonard is woken by the sound of a door shutting firmly. He turns his head to see a glow from under the bathroom door.

In the dim light he can see a well-worn, coverless paperback book on the far bedside table. Next to it is a hairbrush and a drinking glass half-full of water. There is a small stuffed toy sitting by the pillow next to Leonard's head. Leonard's eyes are half-closed as he slides his hand on to the other half of the bed, feeling the residual warmth, smiling.

He props himself up on one arm, rubs his eyes and reaches over to the small green alarm clock, straining to read its numbers in the dim light. He breathes heavily, sleepily and shuts his eyes for a second, utterly content.

LEONARD
(*about to tell his companion something*)

Honey?

The sound of the shower being run. He opens his eyes and looks over to the bathroom door.

(*relaxed*)

Honey? It's late.

He swings his legs over and sits on the edge of the bed. Move in on Leonard's face.

Everything OK?

He looks around with growing unease.

INT. BATHROOM OF LEONARD'S APARTMENT – NIGHT

Trembling, shallow-focus extreme close-ups:

A glass bottle shatters against a tiled floor, bath salts and glass spreading out over the black-and-white tiles.

INT. DISCOUNT INN ROOM 304 — NIGHT

Leonard rises from the bed, staring at the bathroom door.

INT. BATHROOM OF LEONARD'S APARTMENT — NIGHT

Sudden movement glimpsed through a water-beaded clear plastic shower curtain. Mirror shattering.

INT. DISCOUNT INN ROOM 304 — NIGHT

Leonard is at the bathroom door. He taps gently.

INT. BATHROOM OF LEONARD'S APARTMENT — NIGHT

The wet plastic shower curtain pulls taut across a gasping, thrashing female face.

INT. DISCOUNT INN ROOM 304 — NIGHT

Leonard knocks again. No answer. He knocks louder, concerned.

> LEONARD
>
> Are you OK in there?!

He grabs the handle, throws open the door.

INT. STEAM-FILLED BATHROOM OF ROOM 304 — NIGHT

A blonde woman in a silk dressing gown, seated on the toilet, looks up from snorting a line of cocaine off a small hand mirror. She giggles as she speaks to Leonard.

> BLONDE
>
> Was it good for you?

Leonard stands in the doorway, shaken. The Blonde realizes that he is not happy.

> Shit. Was I supposed to lock the door?

> LEONARD
>
> No. That would have been worse.

He moves to turn off the shower.

167

I'd like you to leave now.

INT. DISCOUNT INN ROOM 304 – NIGHT – LATER

Leonard, fully clothed, grabs a shopping bag from the closet and does a quick circuit of the room, grabbing various items (the paperback book, hairbrush, alarm clock, stuffed toy) and stuffing them into the bag.

EXT. DISCOUNT INN – NIGHT

Leonard comes out of room 304, grim-faced, carrying the shopping bag. He goes to his Jaguar and gets in.

CUT TO:

INT. MOTEL ROOM 21 – NIGHT [BLACK-AND-WHITE SEQUENCE]

Leonard (boxers, bandaged arm) dips the needle into the ink reservoir and punctures the skin of his thigh, talking on the phone.

> LEONARD
> Well, sir, that would certainly be in keeping with some of my own discoveries. Yeah, I was hoping to get more on the drugs angle. Hang on a second.

He drops the needle/pen, pulls a large file out of his sports bag and opens it on the bed.

> The police report mentioned the drugs found in the car outside my house. The car was stolen, but his prints were all over it, along with some of his stuff. And I think there's something . . .
> (*flips through pages*)
> Something about a syringe . . .
> (*flips pages, confused*)
> I've got a copy of the police report. It has lots of information, but with my condition, it's tough. I can't really keep it all in mind at once.

He looks at the back of the file, where he has written a list of 'CONCLUSIONS'.

> I have to keep summarizing the different sections . . .

He flips back to the front page. On it there is a handwritten note:
'MISSING PAGES: 14–17, 19, 23 . . .'.

> Yeah, and there's pages missing . . . I guess I've been trying to
> log them all.
> > (*listens, smiles*)
> The police gave me the report themselves. I dealt with them a
> lot in my insurance job, and I had friends in the department.
> They must have figured that if I saw the facts of the case, then
> I would stop believing that we needed to find John G.

He flips to the back page to look at his handwritten conclusions.

> They weren't even looking for John G. The stuff they found in
> the car just fit in with what they believed had happened, so
> they didn't chase any of it up.

EXT. DISCOUNT INN — DAY [COLOUR SEQUENCE]

*Leonard pulls up in the Jaguar, checks the name against a note written
on a beer mat, and heads into the office.*

*He comes out of the office, gets a sports bag from the Jaguar, then takes
a Polaroid of the entrance and heads for room 304.*

INT. DISCOUNT INN ROOM 304 — DAY

*Leonard enters the unoccupied room, flapping the Polaroid photo. He
sifts through his sports bag, pulls out a pen and writes the motel's
address on the picture.*

*With well-practiced, efficient movements, Leonard removes his wall
chart from the sports bag, unrolls it, sticks it to the wall. He takes a
stack of Polaroids out of the sports bag and works through them, considering each new picture and finding its proper place on the chart like
someone playing solitaire.*

> LATER:

Leonard flips through the Yellow Pages, looking under 'Escort Services'.

> LATER:

Leonard is on the phone.

                                LEONARD
None? OK, blonde. Yeah, blonde is fine. Discount Inn, 304.
Leonard.

LATER:

Leonard opens the door to the Blonde.

LATER:

*The Blonde is looking curiously at the chart, drink in hand. Leonard is
in the chair.*

                                BLONDE
Well, what then?

                                LEONARD
It's simple, you just go to the bathroom.

The Blonde turns, surprised. Leonard smiles, embarrassed.

No, you just go *into* the bathroom. We go to bed, you wait till
I fall asleep, then you go into the bathroom and slam the
door.

                                BLONDE
Slam it?

                                LEONARD
Just loud enough to wake me up.

                                BLONDE
That's it?

                                LEONARD
That's it.

*He gets up, pulls a paper shopping bag out of the closet and hands it to
the Blonde.*

But first I need you to put these things around.

The Blonde looks confused.

Just pretend these things are yours, and this is your bedroom.

The Blonde pulls a bra out of the bag.

> BLONDE

Should I wear it?

> LEONARD

No. Just leave the stuff lying around as if it were yours. Like you just took it off or something.

> BLONDE

Whatever gets you off.

She pulls the hairbrush out of the bag. She moves to brush her hair with it, but Leonard stops her.

> LEONARD

No! No, don't use it, you, I mean it's . . . you just have to put it where you would if it were yours.

The Blonde sees the black hair stuck in the brush.

INT. DISCOUNT INN ROOM 304 – NIGHT

The lights are off. The Blonde and Leonard are lying side by side in bed.

The Blonde checks to see that Leonard is asleep, then slips out of bed. She grabs her purse, then opens the bathroom door. She looks back at Leonard, asleep. She moves into the bathroom and shuts the door firmly, making a loud bang.

Leonard's eyes open.

INT. MOTEL ROOM 21 – DAY [BLACK-AND-WHITE SEQUENCE]

Leonard (boxers, bandaged arm) tattoos himself as he talks on the phone. So far he has tattooed:
'FACT 5.'.

> LEONARD

The drugs stashed in the car doesn't ring true for me.

He consults his file card, which says:
'TATTOO: ACCESS TO DRUGS'.

The police figure the guy was an addict needing money to

score, but I'm not convinced. He's not gonna be breaking in
when he's still got a stash that big.
                    (*listens*)
I think John G. left it or planted it.
                    (*listens*)
Well, it was a lot for one guy's personal use.
                    (*listens*)
How do you know that?
                    (*listens, checks report*)
Right, that's true. It fits.
                    (*listens*)
Too much for personal use, so he deals.

He takes his pen and alters his file card to read:
'TATTOO: FACT 5. DRUG DEALER'.

He picks up the needle/pen and continues his tattoo.

EXT. NATALIE'S HOUSE – DAY [COLOUR SEQUENCE]

The car alarm of the Jaguar is sounding.

Leonard exits, walks to the car and gets in, switching off the alarm.

                    TEDDY (O.S.)
You should lock a car as nice as this.

He is in the passenger seat. Leonard, startled, grabs him by the throat.

                    LEONARD
Who the fuck are you?

                    TEDDY
                    (*gasping*)
Teddy. Your buddy.

                    LEONARD
Prove it.

                    TEDDY
                    (*gasping*)
Sammy. Remember Sammy. You told me about Sammy.

Leonard lets him go.

LEONARD

What are you doing in my car?

Teddy is now wearing his big grin, rubbing his neck.

TEDDY

Sense of humour went with the memory, huh? You know why you're still here, don't you?

LEONARD

Unfinished business.

TEDDY

Lenny, as a buddy, let me inform you. Your business here is very much finished. You're still here because of Natalie.

LEONARD

Who's she?

Teddy chuckles.

TEDDY

Whose house do you think you just walked out of?

Leonard looks at the house. Teddy motions towards Leonard's pockets.

Take a look at your pictures. I bet you got one of her.

Leonard pulls out his Polaroids and flips through them. He pauses at the one of Natalie. Teddy swipes it out of his hands to get a better look at the blurred image of Natalie turning in a doorway.

Great shot, Lenny.

He flips the photo over. There is nothing on the back. He hands it back to Leonard.

You wanna make a note that you can't trust her.

LEONARD

Why's that?

TEDDY

Because she'll have taken one look at your clothes and your car and started thinking of ways to turn the situation to her advantage. She's already got you staying with her, for fuck's sake. You can't stay with her. Let me give you the name of a motel.

He starts looking for a piece of paper.

Good thing I found you. She's bad news.

LEONARD

What do you mean 'bad news'?

TEDDY

She's involved with these drug dealers.

He opens the glove compartment, finding a stack of beer mats from a local bar called Ferdy's.

See these? That's the bar where she works. Her boyfriend's a drug dealer. She'd take orders for him, arrange meets. He'd write messages on these, then leave it on the bar. She'd drop replies when she served him drinks.

LEONARD

Why should I care?

Teddy starts writing on the beer mat.

TEDDY

She's gonna use you. To protect herself.

LEONARD

From who?

TEDDY

Guys who'll come after her. Guys who'll want to know what happened to her boyfriend. They'll want to make somebody pay. Maybe she'll try and make it you.

LEONARD

Yeah, well, maybe she'll make it you. Is that it? You worried she'll use me against you?

TEDDY

She couldn't.

LEONARD

Why not?

TEDDY

(*grins*)

She has no idea who I am.

LEONARD

Why are you following me?

TEDDY

I'm trying to help you. I knew she'd get her claws into you.
She doesn't know anything about your investigation, so when
she offers to help you, it'll be for her own reasons. Why
would I lie? Do not go back to her. Take out a pen, write
yourself a note, do not trust her.

*Leonard takes out his pen, places the picture of Natalie face down on
the dash and writes on the white strip on the back:*
'DON'T TRUST HER'.

LEONARD

Happy now?

TEDDY

I won't be happy until you leave town.

LEONARD

Why?

TEDDY

How long do you think you can hang around here before
people start asking questions?

LEONARD

What sort of questions?

TEDDY

The sort of questions you should be asking yourself.

LEONARD

Like what?

TEDDY

Like how'd you get this car? That suit?

LEONARD

I have money.

175

TEDDY

From what?

LEONARD

My wife's death. I used to work in insurance, we were well covered.

TEDDY

So in your grief you wandered into a Jaguar dealership?

Leonard says nothing. Teddy laughs.

You haven't got a clue, have you? You don't even know who you are.

LEONARD

Yes, I do. I don't have amnesia. I remember everything about myself up until the incident. I'm Leonard Shelby, I'm from San Fran–

TEDDY

That's who you *were*, Lenny. You don't know who you *are*, who you've become since the incident. You're wandering around, playing detective . . . and you don't even know how long ago it was.

He reaches out to Leonard's lapel, and gently opens his jacket to reveal the label.

Put it this way. Were you wearing designer suits when you sold insurance?

Leonard looks down at his suit, then back to Teddy.

LEONARD

I didn't sell –

TEDDY

I know, you investigated. Maybe you need to apply some of your investigative skills to yourself.

LEONARD

Yeah, well, thanks for the advice.

TEDDY

Don't go back in there. There's a motel out of town.

He hands Leonard the beer mat and gets out of the car.

It's been fun, Lenny.

He walks off. Leonard pulls his Polaroids out of his pocket and finds the one of Teddy. He places it on the dash, face up, next to the one of Natalie, which is still face down on the dash. Leonard reads the message he has written on the back of Natalie's picture:
'DON'T TRUST HER'.

He flips Teddy's picture over, like a croupier turning a card at black-jack. On the back it says:
'DON'T BELIEVE HIS LIES'.

Leonard purses his lips in surprised frustration. He grabs his pen and scribbles on the back of Natalie's picture, obliterating the words:
'DON'T TRUST HER'.

He flips Natalie's picture over and considers her blurred image. He looks up at her house, then picks up the beer mat, reading the address Teddy has given him.

LEONARD

Fuck it. I need my own place.

He starts the engine.

EXT. DISCOUNT INN — DAY

Leonard pulls up in his Jaguar, checks the name of the motel against the note written on the beer mat, then heads into the office to check in.

He comes out of the office, takes a Polaroid of the front of the motel, and heads for room 304.

INT. MOTEL ROOM 21 — DAY [BLACK-AND-WHITE SEQUENCE]

Leonard (boxers, bandaged arm) talks on the phone. He presses the needle/pen against his thigh, working on a 'D'.

LEONARD

I can't blame the cops for not taking me seriously. This is a dif-

177

ficult condition for people to understand. I mean, look at
Sammy Jankis. His own wife couldn't deal with it.
> (*listens*)

I told you about how she tried to get him to snap out of it?
> (*listens*)

It got much worse than that. Eventually Sammy's wife came to
see me at the office and I found out all kinds of shit.
> (*listens*)

She knew that I was the one who had built the case for
Sammy faking it.

INT. LEONARD'S OFFICE – DAY

*Leonard, in a cheap suit and tie, gets up from behind his desk to
shake hands with Mrs Jankis. They talk, Leonard nodding as he listens. Mrs Jankis is crying.*

> LEONARD (V.O.)
>
> She told me about life with Sammy, how she'd treated him. It
> had got to the point where she'd get Sammy to hide food all
> around the house, then stop feeding him to see if his hunger
> would make him remember where he'd hidden the stuff. She
> wasn't a cruel person, she just wanted her old Sammy back.

The tearful Mrs Jankis gives Leonard a determined look.

> MRS JANKIS
>
> Mr Shelby, you know all about Sammy and you decided that
> he was faking –

> LEONARD
>
> Mrs Jankis, the company's position isn't that Sammy is 'fak-
> ing' anything, just that his condition can't be shown –

> MRS JANKIS
>
> I'm not interested in the company position, Mr Shelby. I want
> to know your honest opinion about Sammy.

> LEONARD
>
> We shouldn't even be talking this way while the case is still
> open to appeal.

MRS JANKIS

I'm not appealing the decision.

LEONARD

Then why are you here?

MRS JANKIS

Mr Shelby, try and understand. When I look into Sammy's
eyes, I don't see some vegetable, I see the same old Sammy.
What do you think it's like for me to suspect that he's imagin-
ing this whole problem? That if I could just say the right thing
he'd snap out of it and be back to normal? If I knew that my
old Sammy was truly gone, then I could say goodbye and start
loving this new Sammy. As long as I have doubt, I can't say
goodbye and move on.

LEONARD

Mrs Jankis, what do you want from me?

MRS JANKIS

I want you to forget the company you work for for thirty seconds, and tell me if you really think that Sammy is faking his
condition.

Leonard plays with his letter opener, thinking.

I need to know what you honestly believe.

LEONARD
(looks at Mrs Jankis)

I believe that Sammy should be physically capable of making
new memories.

MRS JANKIS

Thank you.

INT. MOTEL ROOM 21 – DAY

LEONARD

She seemed to leave happy. I thought I'd helped her.

He puts the needle/pen down and wipes blood from his new,
homemade tattoo, which says:
'FACT 5. DRUG DEALER'.

I thought she just needed some kind of answer. I didn't think it was important to her what the answer was, just that she had one to believe.

He notices the bandage on his left arm. He starts fiddling with the tape, peeling back the corners.

CUT TO:

INT. NATALIE'S LIVING ROOM — DAY [COLOUR SEQUENCE]

Leonard sifts through the papers on the desk, agitated. He hears a car door slam. He looks out of the window to see Natalie getting out of her car.

She turns and comes towards the front door. Her face is swollen and bleeding.

Leonard opens the door for her. She rushes past him.

                    LEONARD
What happened?

Natalie, intensely agitated, fumbles with things in her purse.

                    NATALIE
What does it look like?!

She turns to Leonard so that he can see the full extent of her injuries. Her eye is swelling up and her lip is split.

He beat the shit out of me.

                    LEONARD
Who?

                    NATALIE
Who?! Fuck, Leonard! Dodd! Dodd beat the shit out of me.

She flings her purse to the ground in frustration. She does not know what to do with her hands.

                    LEONARD
Why?

Natalie turns to him, enraged.

NATALIE

Because of you, you fucking idiot! Because I did what you told me! Go to him, reason with him, tell him about Teddy! Great fucking idea!

Leonard approaches her, palms out.

LEONARD

Calm down.

Natalie starts to hit Leonard. He takes her arms.

(*softly*)
Take it easy. You're safe now. You're safe.

He sits her down on the couch.

Let's get some ice on your face.

LATER:

Natalie, crying softly, holds a paper towel filled with ice cubes to her swollen cheek while Leonard gently uses a damp paper towel to wipe the blood from her upper lip.

NATALIE

I did exactly what you told me. I went to Dodd and I said that I didn't have Jimmy's money, or any drugs, that this Teddy must have taken everything.

LEONARD

And what did he say?

NATALIE

He didn't believe me. He said that if I don't get him the money tomorrow he's gonna kill me. Then he started hitting me.

LEONARD

Where is he?

NATALIE

What are you gonna do?

LEONARD

I'll go see him.

NATALIE

And?

LEONARD

Give him some bruises of his own and tell him to look for a
guy called Teddy.

NATALIE

He'll kill you, Lenny.

LEONARD
(*smiling*)
My wife used to call me Lenny.

NATALIE

Yeah?

LEONARD

Yeah, I hated it.

NATALIE

This guy's dangerous, let's think of something else.

Leonard takes out a piece of paper, but he cannot find his pen.

LEONARD

I'll take care of it. Just tell me what he looks like, and where I
can find him. Do you have a pen?

Natalie gets a pen out of her purse and hands it to him.

NATALIE

He'll probably find you.

LEONARD

Me? Why would he be interested in me?

NATALIE

I told him about your car.

LEONARD

Why would you do that?

NATALIE

He was beating the crap out of me! I had to tell him something!

Leonard hands Natalie the piece of paper and pen.

> LEONARD
>
> Just write it all down. What he looks like, where I find him.

Natalie hands him a note. It says:
'DODD, MOUNTCREST INN ON 5TH STREET, ROOM 6
PUT HIM ON TO TEDDY OR JUST GET RID OF HIM FOR NATALIE'

Outside, a car alarm starts to sound. Leonard gets up and heads to the door, flipping through his Polaroids.

EXT. NATALIE'S HOUSE – DAY

The Jaguar's car alarm is sounding.

Leonard exits Natalie's house, walks to his Jaguar and gets in, silencing the alarm.

> TEDDY (O.S.)
>
> You should lock a car as nice as this.

Leonard, startled, grabs Teddy by the throat.

> CUT TO:

INT. MOTEL ROOM 21 – DAY [BLACK-AND-WHITE SEQUENCE]

Leonard (boxers, bandage on arm) sits on the edge of the bed, talking on the phone.

> LEONARD
>
> No, she shouldn't have given me that responsibility. Shit, I'm not a doctor, I'm a claims investigator.

He crooks his neck to hold the receiver between ear and shoulder and fiddles with the bandage on his left arm, starting to peel back the tape, trying to look under the cotton pad.

> I suppose, but I've got all sorts of other considerations.

He starts to remove the bandage.

> Legal responsibility, and large financial . . .

He removes the bandage from his left arm, revealing a crude tattoo which says:
'NEVER ANSWER THE PHONE'.

He looks up.

Who is this?

He takes the receiver away from his ear as if the caller has just hung up.

CUT TO:

INT. NATALIE'S LIVING ROOM — DAY [COLOUR SEQUENCE]

Leonard is sitting on the coffee table, relaxed, looking at his Polaroids. Natalie (without bruises) bursts in through the front door, scared.

LEONARD
What's wrong?

NATALIE
Somebody's come. Already.

LEONARD
Who?

NATALIE
Calls himself Dodd.

LEONARD
What does he want?

NATALIE
Wants to know what happened to Jimmy. And his money. He thinks I have it. He thinks I took it.

LEONARD
Did you?

NATALIE
No!

LEONARD
What's this all about?

Natalie looks at him bitterly.

NATALIE

You don't know, do you? You're blissfully ignorant, aren't you?

LEONARD

I have this condition –

NATALIE

I know about your fucking condition, Leonard! I probably know more about it that you do! You don't have a fucking clue about anything else!

LEONARD

What happened?

NATALIE

What happened is that Jimmy went to meet a guy called Teddy. He took a lot of money with him and he didn't come back. Jimmy's partners think I set him up. I don't know whether you know this Teddy or how well –

Leonard is getting frustrated.

LEONARD

Neither do I.

NATALIE

Don't protect him.

LEONARD

I'm not.

NATALIE

Help me.

LEONARD

How?

NATALIE

Get rid of Dodd for me.

LEONARD

What?

NATALIE

Kill him. I'll pay you.

LEONARD

What do you think I am?! I'm not gonna kill someone for money.

NATALIE

What then? Love? What would you kill for? For your wife, right?

LEONARD

That's different.

NATALIE

Not to me! I wasn't fucking married to her!

LEONARD

Don't talk about my wife.

NATALIE

I can talk about whoever the fuck I want! You won't even remember what I say! I can tell you that your wife was a fucking whore and we can still be friends!

Leonard stands up.

LEONARD

Calm down.

NATALIE

That's easy for you to say! You can't get scared, you don't remember how, you fucking idiot!

LEONARD

Just take it easy, this isn't my fault.

NATALIE

Maybe it is! How the fuck would you know?! You don't know a fucking thing! You can't get scared, can you get angry?!

Leonard steps towards her.

LEONARD

Yes.

NATALIE

You pathetic piece of shit. I can say whatever the fuck I want and you won't have a clue, you fucking retard.

LEONARD

Shut the fuck up!

Natalie gets right in his face, grinning.

NATALIE

I'm gonna use you, you stupid fuck. I'm telling you now because I'll enjoy it more if I know that you could stop me if you weren't a freak.

Leonard grabs his Polaroids and finds one of Natalie. He reaches into his pocket for a pen, but cannot find one.

Lost your pen? That's too bad, freak. Otherwise you could've written yourself a little note about how much Natalie hates your retarded guts.

Leonard moves around the room searching for a pen. Natalie follows him, speaking into his ear.

No pens here, I'm afraid. You're never going to know that I called you a retard and your wife a whore.

Leonard turns to face her, barely controlling his anger.

LEONARD

Don't say another fucking word!

NATALIE

About your whore of a wife?

Leonard slaps Natalie. She smiles, then speaks softly.

I read about your problem. You know what one of the causes of short-term memory loss is?

Leonard fumes.

Venereal disease. Maybe your cunt of a wife sucked one too many diseased cocks and turned you into a retard.

Leonard turns away, body tensed, ready to snap. Natalie reaches out to gently brush the hair above his ear with her fingers.

You sad freak, you won't remember any of what I've said, and we'll be best friends, or even lovers.

Leonard spins around, backhanding Natalie on the cheek.

He punches her in the mouth then pushes her to the floor. He stands over her, furious with himself as much as her.

Natalie gets to her feet, and goes to the door. She turns to Leonard. Her face is bloody but she smiles.

See you soon.

She exits. Leonard watches her walk out to her car and get in. She just sits there.

Leonard turns from the window and looks around the room. He grabs at drawers, searching for a pen. He looks back out of the window. Natalie is still sitting in her car. Leonard is sifting through the papers on the desk when he hears a car door slam. He looks out of the window to see Natalie getting out of her car. She turns to walk toward the house. Her face is swollen and bloody.

Leonard opens the door for her.

LEONARD

What happened?

Natalie, intensely agitated, fumbles with things in her purse.

NATALIE

What does it look like?

INT. MOTEL ROOM 21 – DAY [BLACK-AND-WHITE SEQUENCE]

Leonard lies on the bed, in jeans, topless. He reaches for the ringing phone with his left arm. As his hand reaches the receiver, he reads the tattoo on his arm which says:
'NEVER ANSWER THE PHONE'.

He strokes the tattoo as he lets the phone ring. It stops. He goes to

*the door, opens it and checks the number of the room: 21. He goes
back to the phone, makes a call.*

                    LEONARD
Front desk? Burt, right. Well, this is Mr Shelby in room 21. I
don't want any calls, none at all, got it? Thanks.

CUT TO:

EXT. NATALIE'S HOUSE — DAY [COLOUR SEQUENCE]

*Leonard's Jaguar pulls up. Leonard and Natalie (without bruises) get
out. Leonard is carrying his sports bag.*

INT. NATALIE'S LIVING ROOM — DAY

Natalie leads Leonard in, self-conscious about her messy living room.

                    NATALIE
You can just crash out on the couch. You'll be comfortable.

Leonard nods and stands awkwardly.

    Uh, take a seat.

*Leonard smiles and sits down in a chair. Natalie clears things off the
coffee table. Leonard unzips his bag and looks through his things,
pulling out his file.*

    So how long you think it's gonna take you?

Leonard raises his eyebrows.

    You told me you were looking for the guy who killed your
    wife.

                    LEONARD
                (consulting file)
Depends on if he's here in town. Or if he's moved on. See,
I've got all this —

                    NATALIE
    Can I ask you something?

Leonard nods.

                    189

If you've got all this information, how come the police
haven't found him for you?

                    LEONARD
They're not looking for him.

                    NATALIE
Why not?

*Leonard runs his finger down the list of conclusions on the back of his
file.*

                    LEONARD
They don't think he exists.

Natalie looks confused.

I told them what I remembered. I was asleep, something
woke me up . . .

CUT TO FLASHBACK:

INT. BEDROOM OF LEONARD'S APARTMENT – NIGHT

*Leonard opens his eyes. He slides his hand over to the empty space on
the bed beside him, feeling the sheet.*

                    LEONARD (V.O.)
Her side of the bed was cold. She'd been out of bed for a
while.

He sits up in bed, listening.

INT. LEONARD'S HALLWAY WITH WOODEN FLOORS AND HIGH
CEILINGS – NIGHT

*We move down the hall towards a closed door. Shadows and light play
across the floorboards from the gap under the door. An ominous rumbling builds.*

INSERT QUICK CUTS:

Extreme close-ups:

*A glass bottle smashes against ceramic tiles. A mirror smashes. Flesh
hits tiled floor.*

INT. BEDROOM OF LEONARD'S APARTMENT — NIGHT

Leonard takes a gun down from the top of the bedroom closet, then quietly makes his way into the corridor.

INT. BATHROOM OF LEONARD'S APARTMENT — NIGHT

Leonard kicks the door open, revealing two figures struggling on the floor of a bathroom.

Close-up of a woman's face, wrapped in the wet clear plastic shower curtain, struggling to breathe.

Close-up of a baseball cap-covered head turning to reveal a face covered by a dirty white cotton mask.

Close-up of a gloved hand drawing a pistol from the back of a waistband.

A shot rings out and the white cotton mask is blown into red, the masked man falling off the struggling woman. Leonard stands in the doorway, smoking gun in hand. He is hit hard from behind by an unseen assailant, who grabs him by the hair and throws his head into the mirror, shattering it. Leonard drops to the floor.

An extreme close-up of a woman's staring eyes, seen through water-beaded, blood-spattered clear plastic.

The eyes blink and we white out.

FADE DOWN FROM WHITE TO:

INT. NATALIE'S LIVING ROOM — DAY

LEONARD

There had to be a second man. I was struck from behind, I remember. It's about the last thing I do remember. But the police didn't believe me.

NATALIE

How did they explain what you remembered? The gun and stuff?

LEONARD
(*points at conclusions on back of file*)
John G. was clever. He took the dead man's gun and replaced

it with the sap that he'd hit me with. He left my gun and left the getaway car. He gave the police a complete package. They found a sap with my blood on it in the dead man's hand, and they only found my gun. They didn't need to look for anyone else. I was the only guy who disagreed with the facts, and I had brain damage.

Natalie watches him.

NATALIE

You can stay here for a couple of days if it'll help.

LEONARD

Thank you.

NATALIE

I've got to get back for the evening shift, so make yourself at home, watch TV, whatever. Just grab a blanket and pillow off the bed. I never need them all anyway.

Leonard nods. Natalie heads for the door.

LEONARD

Oh, one thing.

Natalie turns. Leonard snaps her picture with his Polaroid camera. He lowers the camera and smiles.

Something to remember you by.

Natalie smiles unconvincingly, perturbed, and exits. Leonard sits down on the couch and writes 'NATALIE' on the white strip under her photo as it develops into the blurred image of Natalie which we have seen before. He takes out his other Polaroids, flipping through them.

LATER:

Leonard watches commercials on TV. He notices the tattoo on his hand ('REMEMBER SAMMY JANKIS'), then switches the TV off. He starts to examine his Polaroids.

Natalie bursts through the door, worried.

What's wrong?

NATALIE

Somebody's come. Already.

CUT TO:

INT. MOTEL ROOM 21 – DAY [BLACK-AND-WHITE SEQUENCE]

There is a knock at the door. Leonard pulls on his long-sleeved plaid work shirt, goes to the door and opens it. Burt is standing there.

BURT

Leonard, it's Burt, from the front desk.

LEONARD

Yeah?

BURT

I know you said you didn't want any calls . . .

LEONARD

That's right, I did, didn't I?

BURT

Yeah, but there's a call for you from this guy. He's a cop.

LEONARD

A cop?

BURT

And he says you're gonna wanna hear what he's got to say.

LEONARD
(*shakes head*)

I'm not too good on the phone. I need to look people in the eye when I talk to them.

Burt shrugs, then walks off.

CUT TO:

INT. FERDY'S BAR – DAY [COLOUR SEQUENCE]

Leonard sits at a booth looking through his Polaroids. A drunk with shaky hands sits at the bar. Natalie (without bruises) is working behind the bar. She tops up a silver tankard with beer, brings it over and sets it in front of Leonard, smiling.

                              NATALIE
        On the house.

                              LEONARD
        Thanks.

Natalie watches in fascination as Leonard drinks from the mug. The drunk is giggling.

                              NATALIE
                           (*fascinated*)
        You really do have a problem. Just like that cop said.

Leonard looks at Natalie, confused.

        Your condition, I mean.

                              LEONARD
                            (*shrugs*)
        Nobody's perfect.

Natalie leans in close, studying Leonard, looking him over.

                              NATALIE
        What's the last thing you remember?

Leonard looks at her.

CUT TO FLASHBACK:

INT. BATHROOM OF LEONARD'S APARTMENT— NIGHT

An extreme close-up, from floor level, of a woman's staring eyes seen through water-beaded, blood-spattered clear plastic.

The eyes blink.

INT. FERDY'S BAR — DAY

Leonard looks at Natalie.

                              LEONARD
        My wife.

NATALIE

Sweet.

LEONARD

Dying.

NATALIE

What?

LEONARD

I remember my wife dying.

Natalie picks up the silver tankard from the table.

NATALIE

Let me get you a fresh glass. I think this one was dusty.

INT. MOTEL ROOM 21 – DAY [BLACK-AND-WHITE SEQUENCE]

Leonard, in boxers and long-sleeved plaid work shirt, lies on the bed, trying to ignore the ringing phone. He rubs his tattoo: 'NEVER ANSWER THE PHONE'. The phone goes quiet.

He hears a noise, and turns to see an envelope sliding underneath the door. He gets off the bed and picks it up. It is addressed: 'LEONARD'. He opens it and removes a Polaroid. The photo of himself, bare-chested, tattooed and grinning maniacally, pointing to the bare area of skin above his heart. Leonard stares at it, disturbed. Underneath the photo is written:
'TAKE MY CALL'.

The phone rings.

CUT TO:

INT. JAGUAR PARKED IN PARKING LOT OF FERDY'S BAR – DAY
[COLOUR SEQUENCE]

Leonard sits, studying his Polaroids. A metallic howl makes him glance up and he sees the lid of a dumpster bang shut. He puts his Polaroids in his pocket and examines the beer mat with the message: 'COME BY AFTERWARDS, NATALIE'.

INT. FERDY'S BAR ON MAIN STREET — DAY

Leonard enters and sits at the bar a couple of places down from a filthy, toothless drunk. Natalie (without bruises) appears in front of him. Leonard looks up at Natalie without recognition. She eyes him coldly, staring at his clothes.

> LEONARD
>
> Beer, please.

> NATALIE
> (*apprehensive*)
>
> What do you want?

> LEONARD
>
> A BEER, please.

> NATALIE
>
> Don't just waltz in here dressed like that and order a beer.

Leonard looks over to the filthy drunk, then back at Natalie.

> LEONARD
>
> There's a dress code?

> NATALIE
>
> What are you here for?

> LEONARD
>
> I'm meeting someone called Natalie.

> NATALIE
>
> Well, that's me.

> LEONARD
>
> Oh. But haven't we met before?

Natalie slowly shakes her head. Leonard is confused.

> So why am I here?

> NATALIE
>
> You tell me.

LEONARD

I don't remember. See, I have no short-term memory. It's not amnesia –

NATALIE

You're the memory guy?

LEONARD

How do you know about me?

NATALIE

My boyfriend told me about you.

LEONARD

Who's your boyfriend?

NATALIE

(*beat*)

Jimmy Grantz. Know him?

Leonard shrugs.

Well, it seems like Jimmy knows you. He told me about you. Said you were staying over at the Discount. Then, just this evening, this cop comes in here looking for you. Looking for a guy who couldn't remember stuff, who'd forget how he got here or where he was going. I told him we get a lot of guys like that in here.

Leonard does not find this funny.

LEONARD

Chronic alcoholism *is* one cause of short-term memory loss.

NATALIE

Are you Teddy?

LEONARD

My name's Leonard.

NATALIE

Did Teddy send you?

LEONARD

I don't know.

197

Natalie stares at him. Her look softens, becoming almost pleading.

                    NATALIE
What's happened to Jimmy?

                    LEONARD
I don't know. I'm sorry.

                    NATALIE
You have no idea where you've just come from? What you've
just done?

Leonard shakes his head.

                    LEONARD
I can't make new memories. Everything fades, nothing sticks.
By the time we finish this conversation, I won't remember
how it started, and the next time I see you I won't know that
I've ever met you before.

                    NATALIE
So why did you come here?

Leonard pulls the beer mat out of his pocket and hands it to Natalie.

                    LEONARD
Found it in my pocket.

Natalie takes it, staring at it, emotional.

                    NATALIE
                    (*quietly*)
Your pocket.

*She retreats down the bar to attend to a customer, eyeing Leonard sus-
piciously as he pulls out his Polaroids.*

LATER:

*Leonard hears a hocking sound and looks over to see the filthy drunk
spitting a blob of sticky phlegm into a silver tankard which Natalie
holds across the bar. She smiles.*

Bar bet.

Leonard shakes his head and looks down. He hears a snort and glances over again. The drunk is pushing his finger against one nostril, whilst blowing snot out of the other into the tankard. Natalie smiles again.

For a lot of money.

She approaches with the tankard.

Care to contribute?

Leonard shakes his head, disgusted. Natalie waves the tankard in his face.

Come on, proceeds are going to charity.

Leonard drops a tidy blob of spit into the beer, shakes his head, revolted. Natalie places the mug on the bar in front of the stool next to Leonard's. She takes a long-handled spoon and stirs it vigorously. Leonard grabs his Polaroids and moves over to a booth.

Natalie brings over the tankard and places it in front of him, smiling.

On the house.

LEONARD
Thank you.

He raises the tankard to his lips.

CUT TO:

INT. MOTEL ROOM 21 — DAY [BLACK-AND-WHITE SEQUENCE]

Leonard, holding the Polaroid of himself, stares at the ringing phone. He picks up the receiver.

LEONARD
(*anxious*)
What do you want?
(*listens*)
I know you're a cop, but what do you want? Did I do something wrong?
(*frightened*)
No, but I can't remember things I do. I don't know what I just did. Maybe I did something wrong, did I do something wrong?

He paces.

I dunno – something bad. Maybe I did something bad.

EXT. ALLEYWAY BEHIND TATTOO PARLOUR – DAY [COLOUR SEQUENCE]

Leonard drops from a window, gains his balance and hurries to his Jaguar, which is parked on the street by the mouth of the alley. He slips into the car, closes the door gently, starts the engine and speeds away.

INT./EXT. JAGUAR PARKED OUTSIDE FERDY'S – DAY

Leonard reaches into his jacket pocket and pulls out a round piece of cardboard. It is a beer mat with the name of a local bar: 'Ferdy's'. There is a message written on it:
'COME BY AFTERWARDS, NATALIE'.

Leonard looks up at the doorway of the bar, then pulls the car around into the parking lot. Natalie is standing by a dumpster, heaving a trash bag into it. She watches the car pull up, unable to see the driver. Natalie casually knocks on the passenger-side window. Leonard lowers the window and Natalie leans down.

NATALIE
(*casual*)

Hey, Jimmy –

She stares at Leonard, confused.

I'm sorry, I . . . I thought you were someone else.

She backs away from the car, perturbed. Just before she disappears around the corner, she tips the lid of the dumpster, letting it fall with a metallic howl and a bang.

INT. MOTEL ROOM 21 – DAY [BLACK-AND-WHITE SEQUENCE]

Leonard talks on the phone, worried.

LEONARD
No, Officer, but with my condition, you don't know anything . . . you feel angry, guilty, you don't know why. You could do something terrible and not have the faintest idea ten minutes later. Like Sammy. What if I've done something like Sammy?!

(*listens*)

I didn't tell you? Didn't I tell you what happened to Sammy and his wife?!

(*listens*)

Mrs Jankis came to my office and asked my honest opinion about Sammy's condition.

INT. LEONARD'S OFFICE – DAY

Mrs Jankis is seated across the desk from Leonard. She gets up to leave. Leonard just sits there.

LEONARD (V.O.)

I never said he was faking. Just that his condition was mental, not physical. She seemed satisfied; she just said 'Thanks' and got up to leave. I found out later that she went home and gave Sammy his final exam.

INT. JANKIS HOUSE LIVING ROOM – DAY

Sammy watches TV commercials. Mrs Jankis watches him.

MRS JANKIS

Sammy, it's time for my shot.

Sammy looks up, smiling, glad to help. He goes into the kitchen and comes back with a bottle of insulin, a syringe and a cotton swab.

He carefully prepares the injection and Mrs Jankis offers him her arm.

LEONARD (V.O.)

She knew beyond doubt that he loved her, so she found a way to test him.

Sammy injects the insulin, then withdraws the needle, smiles reassuringly at his wife and goes back into the kitchen.

Mrs Jankis watches him flipping through the channels, looking for commercials.

She sets her watch back by fifteen minutes.

MRS JANKIS

Sammy, it's time for my shot.

Sammy looks up, smiling, glad to be able to help. He goes into the kitchen and comes back with the bottle of insulin, the syringe and a new cotton swab.

He carefully prepares the injection and Mrs Jankis offers him her other arm. Sammy injects the insulin, then looks up at her and smiles.

Sammy watches TV. Mrs Jankis sets her watch back by fifteen minutes.

Sammy, it's time for my shot.

Sammy looks over from the TV, smiling, glad to be able to help.

Mrs Jankis offers Sammy her leg, and he gives her another shot of insulin, smiling.

LEONARD (V.O.)

She really thought she would call his bluff . . .

Mrs Jankis sets her watch back by fifteen minutes.

. . . or didn't want to live with the things she'd put him through.

Sammy injects her in the stomach.

DISSOLVE TO:

Mrs Jankis unconscious in her chair. Sammy glances over from watching TV commercials, wondering.

He goes to her and takes her hand, nudging her gently.

She went into a coma and never recovered.

Sammy grabs for the phone, dialling frantically.

Sammy couldn't understand or explain what had happened.

Sammy strokes Mrs Jankis's cheek, crying.

INT. CROWDED DAY ROOM OF A NURSING HOME – DAY

Sammy sits watching other patients and nursing staff pass by. He looks at each one with a fresh look of expectant recognition.

> LEONARD (V.O.)
> He's been in a home ever since. He doesn't even know his wife is dead.

INT. MOTEL ROOM 21 – DAY

Leonard strokes the tattoo on his hand.

> LEONARD
> Sammy's brain didn't respond to conditioning, but he was no con man. When his wife looked into his eyes she thought he could be the same as he ever was. When I looked into Sammy's eyes, I thought I saw recognition. We were both wrong.

He looks into the mirror.

> Now I know. You fake it. If you think you're supposed to recognize someone, you pretend to. You bluff it to get a pat on the head from the doctors. You bluff it to seem less of a freak.

EXT. STRIP MALL – DAY [COLOUR SEQUENCE]

The tyres of the Jaguar scream as the car screeches to a halt. Leonard backs the car up and stops in front of a tattoo parlour. He grabs a file card off the dash which says:
'TATTOO: FACT 6. CAR LICENSE NUMBER: SG13 7IU'.

INT. TATTOO PARLOUR – DAY

Leonard (beige suit) enters. A Tattooist is sitting with a magazine, smoking.

> LEONARD
> Didn't know this town had a parlour.

> TATTOOIST
> Every town's got a parlour.

LEONARD

I'd like this on my thigh please.

He hands her a file card. She reads the card, then looks at him. He shrugs.

INT. CURTAINED CUBICLE — TATTOO PARLOUR — DAY — CONTINUOUS

Leonard unbuckles his trousers and starts to pull them down. He stops when he sees his thigh, looking up at the Tattooist.

LEONARD

Promise you won't call me an idiot.

He pulls down his trousers, revealing his scabby, homemade tattoo ('FACT 5: DRUG DEALER'). The Tattooist looks at it.

TATTOOIST
(*shaking her head*)

Idiot.

INT. CURTAINED CUBICLE — TATTOO PARLOUR — DAY — CONTINUOUS

Extreme close-up of the tattooing needle finishing an 'F'.

Wider shows us Leonard sitting with his suit trousers around his ankles in a curtained cubicle. Next to him on the floor is his sports bag full of notes and papers. The Tattooist is tattooing his thigh; Leonard is reading a file, fascinated.

The curtain is thrust open and Teddy pokes his head in.

TEDDY

Hi, Lenny.

The Tattooist turns and looks up at Teddy.

TATTOOIST

It's private back here.

TEDDY

It's all right, we know each other, right, Lenny?

The Tattooist looks to Leonard. He shrugs.

LEONARD

How'd you know I was in here?

TEDDY

The Jaguar's out front. You didn't even bother to put it around the back.

He cranes his neck to see what the tattoo says, but only '6. CA' is visible.

You should have just left town, Lenny. There's tattoo parlours up north.

LEONARD

Guess I wanted to get something down before it slipped my mind.

The tattoo needle buzzes as the Tattooist makes a start on the next letter: a 'R'. Teddy sticks his hand through the curtain.

TEDDY

Gimme the keys. I'll move the car.

Leonard watches Teddy.

LEONARD

It'll be all right for a minute.

Teddy shrugs. The Tattooist looks up at him.

TATTOOIST

Wait out there.

Teddy goes back through the curtain. He pops his head back through the curtain.

TEDDY

Lenny, I'll be back in a minute. I've got to get you some stuff.

INT. CURTAINED CUBICLE – TATTOO PARLOUR – DAY – MOMENTS LATER

The buzzing of the tattoo needle stops. Leonard looks down at his thigh. It says:
'FACT 6. CAR LICENSE NUMBER: SG13 7IU'.

INT. TATTOO PARLOUR — DAY — MOMENTS LATER

Leonard exits the curtained cubicle, buckling his belt. Teddy is waiting for him with a plastic bag. Leonard pays the Tattooist. Teddy looks at her.

> TEDDY

Give us a minute, will ya?

She shrugs and heads into the back. Teddy watches her go, then turns to Leonard, conspiratorial.

We've got to get you out of here.

> LEONARD

Why?

> TEDDY

Why? Come on, Leonard, we talked about this. It's not safe for you to be walking around like this.

> LEONARD

Why not?

> TEDDY

Because that cop's looking for you. We need to get you a change of identity. Some new clothes and a different car should do for now. Put these on.

Teddy offers the bag of clothes. Leonard refuses it.

> LEONARD

What cop?

> TEDDY

This bad cop. He checked you into the Discount Inn. Then he's been calling you for days, sticking envelopes under your door, telling you shit.

> LEONARD

Envelopes?

> TEDDY

He knows you're no good on the phone, so he calls you up to bullshit you. Sometimes you stop taking his calls, so he slips something under your door to frighten you into answering your phone again. He's been pretending to help you. Feeding you a line of crap about John G. being some local drug dealer.

LEONARD

How do you know this?

TEDDY

'Cos he fucking told me. He thinks it's funny. He's laughing at you.

LEONARD

How do you know him?

TEDDY

(glances around)
I'm a snitch. He's a cop from out of town looking for information. The local boys put us in touch.

Leonard takes the plastic bag.

LEONARD

What did he want to know from you?

TEDDY

He wanted to know all about Jimmy Grantz.

LEONARD

Who?

TEDDY

Jimmy's a drug dealer. This cop wanted to know all about how he sets up deals, shit like that. He's got some score in mind and you're involved. Come on, there's no time to argue – if he knew I was helping you, he'd find a way to kill me. Just get these clothes on. You're gonna take my car and get the fuck out of here.

Leonard heads back into the curtained cubicle with the plastic bag of clothes.

INT. CURTAINED CUBICLE – TATTOO PARLOUR – DAY – CONTINUOUS

Leonard drops the plastic bag and takes his jacket off. He feels some-

thing in the pocket, sticks his hand in and pulls out a charred Polaroid photograph.

He examines it, puzzled. All that is visible is an arm lying on a floor. He reaches into the other pocket and pulls out his Polaroids, flicking through them until he finds the one of Teddy. He flips it over and checks the back:
'DON'T BELIEVE HIS LIES'.

He reacts with amused relief.

> LEONARD
> *(under his breath)*
> Sneaky fuck. 'Bad cop.' Had me going.

He puts his jacket back on, checks the other pockets. He finds a beer mat for a local bar named Ferdy's. There is a message written on it:
'COME BY AFTERWARDS, NATALIE'.

Leonard sticks it back in his pocket. He peeks through the curtains. Teddy is sitting by the door, waiting. Leonard looks around, notices a window set high in the wall above the padded bench in the cubicle. He climbs on the bench, opens the window and squeezes himself through.

EXT. TATTOO PARLOUR ALLEYWAY — DAY — CONTINUOUS

Leonard drops from the window, regains his balance and hurries to his Jaguar, which is parked on the street by the mouth of the alley.

> CUT TO:

INT. MOTEL ROOM 21 — DAY [BLACK-AND-WHITE SEQUENCE]

Leonard, in boxers and plaid work shirt, sits hunched over the bed-side table, flipping through the file as he talks on the phone.

> LEONARD
> So this Jimmy Grantz deals drugs out of the bar where his girlfriend works. But he'll come to the meet alone.

He looks down at the fresh tattoo on his thigh.
'FACT 5: DRUG DEALER'.

He consults a file which he has drawn from his bag.

I always figured the drugs angle would be the best way to get him. No, Officer, I'm ready. Ready as I'll ever be.
              (*listens*)
You're downstairs now? What do you look like?
              (*listens*)
I'll be right down.

He hangs up the phone and pulls on a pair of scruffy jeans. He grabs his Polaroid camera and puts it over his shoulder.

EXT. DISCOUNT INN – DAY

Leonard exits and heads to the motel office.

INT. DISCOUNT INN OFFICE – DAY

The bell chimes as Leonard enters. Burt is behind the counter. A man stands by the free coffee. The man turns around. It is Teddy, with a big grin.

                    TEDDY

Lenny!

Leonard smiles cautiously and offers his hand.

                    LEONARD

Officer Gammell.

EXT. DISCOUNT INN – DAY

Leonard exits the office, followed by Teddy, and looks through his Polaroids. He finds one of a pick-up truck, spots it in the lot, and walks over to it. He turns around and points his camera at Teddy. Teddy grins wider. Leonard snaps the picture.

                    LEONARD
Something to remember you by.

He lowers the camera and takes out a pen, resting the picture against the truck, about to write on the white strip beneath the developing picture.

I'm sorry – is it Officer or Lieutenant Gammell?

Teddy coughs and looks at the picture.

>   TEDDY
>   Just Teddy. Don't write Gammell, please.

Leonard raises his eyebrows.

> I'm under cover. Here's directions. He'll be heading there now.

He pulls a note out of his pocket and hands it to Leonard.

>   LEONARD
>   You're not coming?

>   TEDDY
>   Wouldn't be appropriate.

Leonard climbs into the truck. Teddy taps on the window.

> Leonard?

Leonard cranks it down. Teddy looks at him with something like fatherly affection.

> Make him beg.

INT./EXT. PICK-UP TRUCK ON STREET – DAY

The pick-up truck speeds along, past strip malls and gas stations, heading into more desolate industrialization.

EXT. DERELICT BUILDING – DAY

The pick-up truck bumps across the railroad tracks, then pulls up in front of the large derelict building. Leonard gets out of the pick-up, looking around.

INT. DERELICT BUILDING – DAY

He heads into the building, down the dimly lit, decaying former hallway, treading carefully on the loose, rotten floorboards. He notices a door at the end of the hallway. He opens the door to see that it leads down to the basement.

He hears a car approaching. He slips into the kitchen and looks out the dirty, broken front windows.

EXT. DERELICT BUILDING – DAY

The Jaguar is approaching fast. It parks next to the pick-up truck and the driver emerges: a young man in his 30s, smartly dressed in beige suit and blue shirt. This is Jimmy, the young man from Natalie's photograph. He looks at the truck, then at the building.

INT. DERELICT BUILDING – DAY

Leonard steps back into the shadows of the crumbling kitchen. Jimmy approaches the doorway, peering into the dark hallway.

> JIMMY

Teddy?!

He steps cautiously inside. Leonard emerges from the kitchen.

> LEONARD

Jimmy?

> JIMMY

What the fuck are you doing here?

> LEONARD

Do you remember me?

> JIMMY
> (*laughs*)

Yeah, I remember you.

> LEONARD

You Jimmy Grantz?

> JIMMY

Expecting any other Jimmys out here, Memory Man? Where the fuck's Teddy?

Leonard comes out of the gloom, stopping in front of Jimmy, studying his face. Leonard has a jack handle in his hand.

Well?

FLASHBACK TO:

INT. BATHROOM OF LEONARD'S APARTMENT – NIGHT

Leonard's Wife, head wrapped in a water-beaded clear plastic shower curtain, thrashing around, gasping for breath.

INT. DERELICT BUILDING – DAY

Leonard hits Jimmy around the head with the jack handle. Jimmy goes down, but struggles as Leonard drags him deeper into the dark hallway. Leonard bends over the groaning Jimmy, frisking him, finding nothing.

                              JIMMY
    You fucking retard, you can't get away with this –

Leonard holds the jack handle above him.

                              LEONARD
    Strip!

Jimmy starts taking off his suit.

                              JIMMY
    You're making a big fucking mistake. My associates are not
    people you want –

                              LEONARD
    Don't say anything else.

                              JIMMY
    I knew I couldn't trust that fuck –

                              LEONARD
    Quiet!

Jimmy drops his shirt.

    Pants, too.

                              JIMMY
    Why?

                              LEONARD
    I don't want blood on them.

JIMMY
(*sudden fear*)
Wait! Did he tell you what I was bringing?

LEONARD
Strip!

JIMMY
Look, there's two hundred grand stashed in the car. Just take it!

Leonard shoves Jimmy to the ground.

LEONARD
You think you can bargain with me?!

JIMMY
Take the money and walk away!

LEONARD
I don't want your fucking money!

JIMMY
What?! What do you want from me?!

Leonard looks up.

INT. LEONARD'S APARTMENT – DAY

Leonard's Wife, smiling.

INT. DERELICT BUILDING – DAY

Leonard is losing it.

LEONARD
I want my fucking life back!

Jimmy swings at Leonard with a broken floorboard, striking his shoulder. The jack handle goes flying. Jimmy swings again, misses. Leonard grabs him, taking him down. The two of them struggle on the floor. Leonard gets on top of Jimmy, choking him. Jimmy tries to speak, but can only make gurgling noises. As Leonard watches Jimmy fight for air, we cut to:

213

INT. BATHROOM OF LEONARD'S APARTMENT – NIGHT

Leonard's Wife thrashes her head from side to side, struggling to breathe through the clear plastic shower curtain.

BACK TO SCENE:

INT. DERELICT BUILDING – DAY

Jimmy's arms thrash, his hand catching Leonard's face, scratching his cheek. Leonard tips his head back and increases his efforts. Jimmy stops struggling. Leonard keeps his hands around Jimmy's throat until he is confident that he is dead.

Leonard breathes as he stands up. He nods to himself with satisfaction. He looks around for his Polaroid camera. He snaps a flash picture of Jimmy's body, and stares intently at the Polaroid as it begins to develop.

We see the image of the strangled Jimmy appear IN COLOUR.

INT. DERELICT BUILDING – DAY – CONTINUOUS [COLOUR SEQUENCE]

Leonard stands above Jimmy's body, examining the picture he has just taken, nodding to himself, catching his breath.

He grabs Jimmy's body by the legs, dragging him back towards the basement. He opens the door and backs down into the darkness, pulling Jimmy behind him.

INT. BASEMENT OF DERELICT BUILDING – DAY – CONTINUOUS

Leonard backs down the stairs, dragging Jimmy's body, head bumping down each step. In the middle of the room, Leonard drops the legs. Moving fast, he pulls the beige suit trousers from the body, and removes his own scruffy jeans and plaid work shirt. He dresses in Jimmy's blue shirt and beige suit. He grabs the Polaroids from his plaid work shirt and sticks them in his suit jacket pocket. He dumps his old clothes on to Jimmy's body. A faint rasping comes from Jimmy's throat. Leonard, frightened, bends down to listen.

JIMMY
(*barely audible rasp*)
Sammy . . . remember Sammy . . .

*Leonard is shocked. Jimmy is silent. The sound of a car outside.
Leonard jumps to his feet.*

INT. KITCHEN OF DERELICT BUILDING – DAY – CONTINUOUS

*Leonard looks out to see Teddy getting out of his grey sedan. Leonard
leafs through his Polaroids, finding the one of Teddy. There is nothing
on the back. He sticks his Polaroids back in his pocket, pausing at the
one of the strangled Jimmy.*

LEONARD (V.O.)
What have I done?

EXT. DERELICT BUILDING – DAY

Leonard emerges to find Teddy trying the Jaguar's doors.

LEONARD
(*distraught*)
Hey! Mister! I need help!

Teddy looks up.

TEDDY
What's wrong?

LEONARD
There's a guy in here, hurt bad! We gotta get him to a doctor!

Teddy moves towards the building. Leonard leads him in.

INT. DERELICT BUILDING – DAY – CONTINUOUS

Teddy follows Leonard down the darkened hall.

LEONARD
(*panicked*)
He might have fallen down the stairs, I don't know, I don't
know what's going on, I'm confused. I have this memory
thing – do I know you?

TEDDY

No. Don't worry, I'm a cop. Everything'll be OK. Is he still breathing?

LEONARD

Maybe. Maybe just.

They go down into the basement.

INT. BASEMENT OF DERELICT BUILDING — DAY — CONTINUOUS

Teddy follows Leonard down the stairs. Jimmy's body, dressed only in boxers, lies in the middle of the floor.

TEDDY

So what were you doing here?

He moves to the body and crouches down to examine it.

LEONARD

I don't know. See, I have this condition.

TEDDY

Well, I hope it's not as serious as his, 'cos this guy's dead.

Leonard cracks Teddy over the head with the floorboard.

FUCK, Lenny! That fucking kills!

LEONARD

Remember me again, huh?

He frisks Teddy, pulling out a gun and a police badge.

You're a cop. A fucking cop.

TEDDY

Yeah, and I helped you find the guy you were looking for –

LEONARD

Get up.

Teddy crawls to his feet, rubbing his head.

INT. DERELICT BUILDING — DAY — CONTINUOUS

Leonard pushes Teddy out of the basement.

TEDDY

I think you've got the wrong idea –

Leonard grabs Teddy.

LEONARD

Who was that? He's not the guy. He *knew* me.

TEDDY

Sure he did. He raped your wife and fucked up your brain.

LEONARD

Bullshit.

TEDDY

His name's James F. Grantz, John G. Check your tattoos.

LEONARD

So what was he bringing the two hundred grand for?

TEDDY

What –

LEONARD

What was it for?

TEDDY

A load of amphetamine I told him I had.

LEONARD

This is a drug deal?!

TEDDY

That, and your thing. Jimmy's your guy, Leonard. I just figured we'd make some money on the side.

LEONARD

But how did he know me?

TEDDY

The Discount Inn, he deals out of there. The guy at the front desk lets him know if anybody comes snooping around. He called Jimmy as soon as you took a picture of that dump.

217

You're using me!

Teddy looks at him, offended.

TEDDY

No!
(*beat*)
You get half.

Leonard throws him against the wall.

LEONARD
He knew about Sammy. Why would I tell him about Sammy?

TEDDY
(*chuckles*)
You tell everyone about Sammy. Everyone who'll listen.
'Remember Sammy Jankis, remember Sammy Jankis.' Great
story. Gets better every time you tell it. So you lie to yourself
to be happy. Nothing wrong with that – we all do. Who cares
if there's a few little things you'd rather not remember?

LEONARD
What the fuck are you talking about?

TEDDY
(*theatrical shrug*)
I dunno . . . your wife surviving the assault . . . her not
believing about your condition . . . the doubt tearing her up
inside . . . the insulin –

LEONARD
That's Sammy, not me! I told you about Sammy –

TEDDY
Like you've told yourself. Over and over. Conditioning yourself to believe. 'Learning through repetition' –

LEONARD
Sammy let his wife kill herself! Sammy ended up in an insti-
tution – !

218

TEDDY

Sammy was a con man. A faker.

LEONARD

I *never* said he was faking! I never said that!

TEDDY

You exposed him for what he was: a fraud.

LEONARD

I was wrong! That's the whole point! Sammy's wife came to me and –

TEDDY

Sammy didn't have a wife.

Leonard freezes, staring at Teddy.

It was *your* wife who had diabetes.

Leonard thinks.

INT. LEONARD'S APARTMENT – DAY

Leonard's Wife sitting on the edge of the bed. She feels a sharp pain and turns to Leonard (just as we have seen before).

LEONARD'S WIFE

Gentle.

Leonard has a syringe in his hand.

INT. DERELICT BUILDING – DAY

Leonard shakes his head, clearing his head of the image.

LEONARD

My wife wasn't diabetic.

TEDDY

Are you sure?

INT. LEONARD'S APARTMENT – DAY

Leonard's Wife on the edge of the bed. She feels a sharp pain and turns to Leonard.

LEONARD'S WIFE

Gentle.

Leonard is playfully pinching her thigh.

INT. DERELICT BUILDING – DAY

Leonard shakes his head, smiling.

LEONARD

She wasn't diabetic. You think I don't know my own wife?
What the fuck is wrong with you?

TEDDY
(*shrugs*)

I guess I can only make you believe the things you want to be
true, huh? Like ol' Jimmy down there.

LEONARD

But he's not the right guy!

TEDDY

He was to you. Come on, Lenny, you got your revenge – just
enjoy it while you still remember.
(*chuckles*)

What difference does it make whether he was your guy or
not?

LEONARD

It makes all the difference.

TEDDY

Why? You're never going to know.

LEONARD

Yes, I will.

TEDDY

No, you won't.

LEONARD

Somehow, I'll know!

TEDDY

You won't remember!

220

LEONARD

When it's done, I'll know! It'll be different!

TEDDY

I thought so too! I was sure you'd remember. But you *didn't*.

Beat. Leonard looks at Teddy, questioning.

(*off look*)

You know, when we found your guy and killed him.

(*off look*)

That's right, the *real* John G. Over a year ago. I helped you find him. He's already dead.

LEONARD

Why do you keep lying to me?

TEDDY

I'm not. I was the cop assigned to your wife's death. I believed you, I thought you deserved the chance for revenge. I helped you find the other guy who was in your bathroom that night. The guy who cracked your skull and fucked your wife. We found him and you killed him. You didn't remember, so I helped you start looking again, looking for the guy you already killed.

LEONARD

So who are you saying he was?

TEDDY

Just some guy. Does it even matter who? I stopped asking myself why a long time ago. No reason, no conspiracy; just bad fucking luck. A couple of junkies, too strung out to realize that your wife didn't live alone. When you killed him, I've never seen you so happy – I was convinced you'd remember. But it didn't stick, like nothing ever sticks. Like *this* won't stick.

Leonard looks at the Polaroid of himself.

That's the picture, right? I took that, right when you did it. Look how happy you are. Before you forgot. I wanted to see that face again.

LEONARD
(*sarcastic*)

Thank you.

TEDDY

Fuck you; I gave you a reason to live and you were more than
happy to help. You lie to yourself! You don't want the truth,
the truth is a fucking coward. So you make up your own
truth. Look at your police file. It was complete when I gave it
to you. Who took the twelve pages out?

LEONARD

You, probably.

TEDDY

No. You took them out.

LEONARD

Why would I do that?

TEDDY

To set yourself a puzzle you won't ever solve. You know how
many towns, how many guys called James G.? Or John G.?
Shit, Leonard, I'm a John G.

LEONARD

Your name's Teddy.

TEDDY
(*chuckles*)

My mother calls me Teddy. I'm John Edward Gammell.
Cheer up, there's a lot of John G.'s for us to find. All you do is
moan. I'm the one that has to live with what you've done. I'm
the one that has to put it all together. You just wander around
playing detective. You're living a dream, kid. A dead wife to
pine for and a sense of purpose to your life. A romantic quest
which you wouldn't end even if I wasn't in the picture.

Leonard sticks the gun in Teddy's face.

LEONARD

I should kill you.

TEDDY

Quit it!

(*brushes the gun away*)

You're not a killer, Lenny. That's why you're so good at it.

Leonard searches Teddy's pockets, still holding the gun on Teddy. He finds Teddy's car keys. He gets off Teddy and moves towards the light.

Hey, where are you going? You know what time it is?

Leonard stares at Teddy, mystified. Teddy grins.

It's beer o'clock. And I'm buying. Our work here is done.

Leonard turns away, and walks out into the light.

EXT. DERELICT BUILDING — DAY — CONTINUOUS

Leonard, in beige suit and blue shirt, comes out into the daylight, throws Teddy's car keys into some bushes, then heads to his pick-up truck and climbs in. Teddy goes to look for his keys in the bushes.

INT. PICK-UP TRUCK — DAY — CONTINUOUS

Leonard opens the revolver and empties the bullets on to the passenger seat. He flips through the photos until he finds the one of the strangled Jimmy.

LEONARD (V.O.)

I'm not a killer . . .

He reaches into his sports bag, grabs a lighter and sparks a flame. He holds the photo in the flame until it catches light, melting and blackening. The flames go out, having destroyed the entire image but for an arm resting on a floor. Leonard sticks the remnants into his jacket pocket. He looks in the rear-view mirror at Teddy, who scrabbles around in the bushes.

. . . but right now I need to be.

Teddy's grey sedan is parked in front of Leonard. Leonard looks at the sedan, then reaches into his sports bag for a pen and a file card. He writes on the file card:

'TATTOO: I'VE DONE IT'.

He looks from the card to Teddy's sedan.

Maybe I'm not finished yet. Maybe I need to be sure that you won't ever use me again.

He rips up the file card and takes out another.

You're a John G.? Fine, then you can be *my* John G.

He writes on the file card:
'TATTOO: FACT 6. CAR LICENSE NUMBER'.

Do I lie to myself to be happy?

He looks up at Teddy's sedan and copies down the licence number, which is: SG13 7IU.

In your case, Teddy . . . yes, I will.

He grabs the sports bag and gets out of the pick-up truck. He goes to the Jaguar and opens the passenger door, dumping his sports bag on to the seat. Teddy sees this and runs over. Leonard walks to the back of the Jaguar and holds up his camera.

TEDDY
Hey! Hey, that's not your car!

Leonard snaps a Polaroid of the Jaguar.

LEONARD
It is now.

TEDDY
You can't just take it!

Leonard unlocks the boot, turning to Teddy as he does so.

LEONARD
Why not?

TEDDY
You just killed the guy who owned it! Somebody'll recognize it!

Leonard pulls Teddy's empty gun out of his pocket.

LEONARD

I'd rather be mistaken for a dead guy than a murderer. I'm gonna hang on to this.

He tosses the gun into the trunk. It lands on piles of banknotes stuffed in the boot. Teddy reacts to the sight of the money. Leonard glances at Teddy, then the money, shakes his head, then slams the trunk. Teddy jogs back to where he was looking for his keys.

INT. JAGUAR – DAY

Leonard starts the engine. Through the rear-view mirror, he stares at Teddy's retreating form. Thinking. Leonard pulls out on to the road.

INT./EXT. ROAD BACK INTO TOWN – DAY

As the Jaguar cruises along, Leonard places the file card on the dash. It says:
'TATTOO: FACT 6. CAR LICENSE NUMBER: SG13 7IU'.

Leonard drives, heading back into town. He looks at his hand on the steering wheel, reading 'REMEMBER SAMMY JANKIS'.

LEONARD (V.O.)

I have to believe in the world outside my own mind. I have to believe that my actions still have meaning, even if I can't remember them. I have to believe that when my eyes are closed, the world's still there.

He closes his eyes, driving blind. Stay on Leonard, not seeing the road ahead, hearing cars whip past.

(*rising tension*)
But do I? Do I believe the world's still there?

Move in on Leonard as cars fly past, horns blaring.

Is it still out there?!
(*beat*)
Yes.

He opens his eyes, straightening up the car, breathing. His eyes dart from the strip malls to the gas stations, as if he is trying to absorb the whole town in a single viewing.

225

We all need mirrors to remind ourselves who we are. I'm no different.

EXT. STRIP MALL — DAY

From the bewildering blur of urban signage, Leonard suddenly glimpses a tattoo parlour in a strip mall. He slams on the brakes.

The tyres scream as the car screeches to a halt and we:

CUT TO BLACK.

LEONARD (V.O.)
Now . . . where was I?

END.

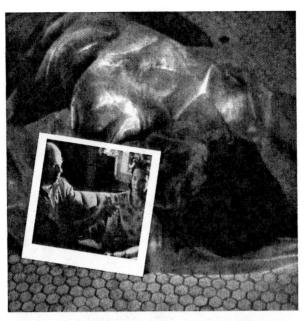

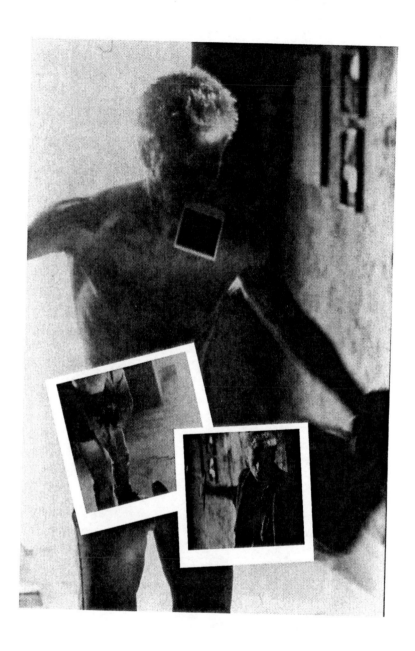

Christopher Nolan with Guy Pearce.

HOW *MEMENTO* BEGAN

CHRIS:

Heading cross-country from Chicago in Dad's old Honda Prelude, we're no further than Wisconsin on the first day when Jonah turns from the passenger seat and tells me he's working on something. Then he gives me his nervous, stalling-for-time smoker's cough that lets me know it's something big. *Ever heard of this condition where you lose your short-term memory?* I think so. *Well, I've got a story about a guy with that. He's in a tattoo parlour getting this tattoo . . .*

Three minutes later my mind's racing. Got a name for it? *'Memento Mori'.* What's that? *On mediaeval gravestones – means remember to die.* Won't work for a film, I think. Great title, I say. Then I tell him he should write it in the first person (doesn't occur to me till much later that I should try and make the film that way, too). I tell him it would make a great film. He agrees: *It's not like these amnesia movies where there's no rules, where the guy doesn't know anything so anything can be true . . .* this is knot-

JONAH:

I tell people that I brought up the story I was working on because we had run out of things to say to each other. But that's not true. I was excited to tell Chris about the story because it was the first good idea I'd had. And because it's always nice to have something interesting to say around your older brothers.

So I think, *What the hell*, because even as I started to write the idea down I knew that it felt as cinematic as literary.

It was a nice day. I'm sure of it. And we were driving my dad's old car from Chicago to Los Angeles. It must have been the second day of driving – we were past Minnesota. I'd guess the windows were open because they were pretty much always open – the car never smelled the same after someone pissed in it one summer in Chicago. I was driving, and I think it was still light out.

And I knew immediately that what I had was pretty good, because my brother was actually paying attention to what I

233

tier – he knows who he was but not who he has become. I start thinking of ways to convince him to let me take it and run with it. Filling up with petrol, I stop myself getting more excited in case he won't let me have a crack at a screenplay.

Now he's driving. I ask if I can write a film from his fledgling short story. The way he says yes I get the idea he was hoping I'd ask. We get excited, throw ideas around: it's got to be cyclical – motel rooms are key . . . The world around us seeps in: the homogeneous American roadside – serial killer Andrew Kunanan adrift – the road – cars . . . I get crazy about a guy who doesn't know how he got his car – maybe he had a different car last time around . . . After a while the conversation turns stale, not helped by the repetition of Jonah's Chris Isaak tape (stuck in the tape player). But something's started.

was saying. He didn't slap his forehead and yell 'Eureka' or anything, but all of a sudden he was actually listening. And while I was explaining my story, I got a slightly sick feeling as I realized how little he'd been listening to me before that.

Pitches and jokes always begin with the same line: 'So there's this guy –'

Fifteen minutes later I was done explaining the idea, and the first thing that occurred to me was the fear that it might be the last good idea I'd have. As soon as I'd let it out, it was gone. My brother was already wrestling it into shape for a screenplay. After that I understood what he meant when he said that once you let an idea out, you can't put it away again.

Both of the above are *true*. The difference between them is what drew me to the world of *Memento*.

Christopher Nolan